Concentration!

How to Focus for Success

Sam Horn

A FIFTY-MINUTE™ SERIES BOOK

CRISP PUBLICATIONS, INC.
Menlo Park, California

CONCENTRATION!
How to Focus for Success

Sam Horn

CREDITS
Editor: **Michael G. Crisp**
Design and Composition: **Interface Studio**
Cover Design: **Carol Harris**
Artwork: **Ralph Mapson**

Copyright © 1991 by Crisp Publications, Inc.
Printed in the United States of America

Distribution to the U.S. Trade:

National Book Network, Inc.
4720 Boston Way
Lanham, MD 20706
1-800-462-6420

Library of Congress Catalog Card Number 90-83476
Horn, Sam
Concentration!
ISBN 1-56052-073-6

This book is printed on recyclable paper with soy ink.
PRINTED WITH SOY INK

PREFACE

People often ask how I got started speaking and writing on the topic of concentration. A few years ago, I was reading the sports section of a major newspaper and noticed that the word ''concentration'' was used six times on one page. In one article, a golfer said it was why she had been able to win a major tournament. In another story, a coach blamed his team's slump on a lack of concentration.

It was intriguing. Experts seemed to agree that concentration was a *key to performance*, often the difference between winning and losing, yet I had never seen any books or seminars on this important topic. I decided to do some research and started interviewing people who were good at what they did. Whether they were surgeons, musicians, athletes, actors, executives or artists, all agreed that concentration played a major role in their success.

What I discovered during my research should be good news for anyone who ever said ''I wish I could concentrate better!'' Believe me, you can! Concentration is not a mystery talent. It is not a gene you're either blessed with or not. It is simply a *skill that everyone can acquire—if* they put their mind to it. (Pun intended!)

This book provides practical, step-by-step strategies you can learn that will help you concentrate better in all areas of your life, at work or at play. You will also discover how to help *other* people acquire this important ability.

This is a *work*book in the real sense of the word. It should be read with pencil in hand. Underline ideas that are particularly relevant for you. If you see an idea and think ''I already know that,'' remember that ''to know and not to do—is not to know at all.'' The point is, ''are you *doing* it? Could it help if you did? Invest the time to answer the questions and complete the exercises and you will comprehend and retain the information because you are *actively* involved. More importantly, by *writing down exactly how you plan to use the ideas presented*, you will be more likely to follow through on your good intentions and take action.

Enjoy! I hope you find this an adventure of self discovery and growth. May this recipe for concentration also serve as a prescription for a healthy and productive life.

Sam Horn

Sam Horn

CONTENTS

PART

I

About Concentration

DEFINITIONS—"WHAT IS CONCENTRATION?"

> *"Any systematic treatment of a subject must first begin with a definition; so that all might understand the object of the inquiry."*—Cicero

Good advice, isn't it? Concentration is a multi-faceted concept. Before discussing *how* you can improve your concentration, it's important first to have some agreement about *what* it is.

This book features five definitions of concentration. Each illustrates a different aspect of this valuable characteristic. After reading each definition, think of a time when you experienced that particular type of concentration. These exercises will demonstrate to you how (sometimes without even being aware of it) you use concentration every day and how it affects all areas of your life.

DEFINITION #1

*Concentration is the **discipline** of **focusing** on a **chosen project** and **ignoring irrelevant** matters.*

There are a couple of key words in this definition. Concentration requires that you *choose a project* from the many competing for your attention. Then you must *discipline* yourself to *ignore all else*. From now on, understand that if you're trying to think about or do several things simultaneously (this is called polyphasic behavior), by definition, you are not concentrating. You'll be diluting your efforts and compromising your performance.

Chris Evert-Lloyd, the famous tennis player, is a great example of someone who learned how to use this type of concentration. When she was practicing under the hot Florida sun, she would force herself to stay on the court hitting balls even when she was tired or when the sun was in her eyes. She trained her mind to totally focus on returning the ball to her opponent's court and ignore everything else. It paid off for her time after time. After winning a major championship, a reporter asked her if the noisy planes flying overhead had bothered her. She looked back at him and replied, "What planes?" She had so totally focused her mind on winning the match that she had become oblivious to "the outside world."

Think of a time you were so focused on what you were doing, you were able to block out distractions. Describe the situation.

_____

_____

DEFINITIONS (Continued)

DEFINITION #2

*Concentration is **interest in action.***

Isn't this eloquent? What is something you love to do? Have you ever gotten so engrossed in reading a good book that you lost track of time? Did you ever get so "caught up" in gardening (or any other hobby like sewing or carpentry) that hours went by and you weren't even aware of them? If so, then you have experienced the joy of this type of concentration. This effortless absorption is almost a "zen-like" state (forgetting the self in the act of uniting with something). A musician described it this way, "I feel embraced by the spirit of music. I feel as though I am plugged into a continuum, like the muse of music. When I am my best, time has stopped and I feel as though I'm not there. It is doing." You don't have to work at this type of concentration, it just happens as a natural result of your total involvement in an activity you enjoy.

A time when I concentrated well and without effort was:

_____

_____

You may be thinking, "It's easy to concentrate when I like what I'm doing. What concerns me are the times I have to concentrate on something and I don't want to. How can I concentrate then?" Don't worry. Chapter 3 outlines how to *arbitrarily provide interest* to enable you to concentrate on boring or tedious projects.

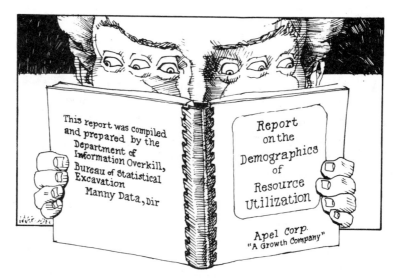

DEFINITION #3

Concentration is the power to give the mind an order and have it obey.

One workshop participant started chuckling after hearing this definition. When asked ''Why?'' he said, ''What's funny is I've always thought of my mind as a spoiled child. I *tell* it what to do, and it ignores me!'' He went on to say, ''That's what concentration is, isn't it? It's **making the mind behave**!''

Can you think of a time when your mind didn't follow orders? Maybe you were supposed to be listening to someone but your mind kept ''escaping to the beach.'' Have you ever been playing a sport but you kept thinking back to something that happened at the office that day, and no matter how much you told yourself to concentrate, you just couldn't keep your mind on your game? It's frustrating, isn't it?

Write down one of those times when your mind wouldn't obey.

_____

_____

DEFINITION #4

//

''Concentration is having the courage to impose on time, people, and events your decision as to what is important and what must come first.''—Peter Drucker

Not sure what that definition means? Picture your desk area. Ask yourself, ''Do I control my environment, or does it control me?'' Do you feel you can't get any work done at your office because people are always interrupting you with questions or problems? Have you ever missed a deadline because a caller just wouldn't get off the phone? Do you feel *external* events are to be blamed for your inability to get things done?

Concentration requires *taking charge* of your work environment instead of being its victim. Later in this book, we'll discuss how to do this *diplomatically* without offending others.

What are two distractions at work that keep you from being as efficient as you would like to be?

_____

_____

DEFINITIONS (Continued)

DEFINITION #5

Concentration is mental tenacity.

This type of concentration can transcend the daily focusing of attention on individual projects and have a more "global" meaning. It involves persevering and accomplishing a desired goal—no matter what! Examples include concentrating on getting a new job, or concentrating on getting elected to a political office.

Have you ever wanted something so much that even when things went wrong, you kept working toward it anyway? One couple decided to build their own home and, unfortunately, Murphy's Law (anything that can go wrong *will*!) took up residence on their lot. A shipment of their materials arrived damaged and they had to re-order everything from scratch. A major subcontractor went bankrupt and didn't finish work for which they had already been paid. It was the wettest winter on record and weeks went by when they could not even work on the house. It would have been easy for them just to give up and quit. Yet this couple didn't because they weren't just *interested* in having their own home, they were *committed*! After two years of frustration, they finally achieved their goal. Every night when they travel up their own driveway, they have the deep satisfaction that comes from working hard to accomplish a desired goal. They have tangible proof of the results of this type of concentration.

When was a time you successfully achieved a goal even after encountering obstacles or difficulties that would have made it easy for you to give up?

Now you know what concentration is, and you have an idea how you've practiced and benefited from it in your life. The next chapter explains the blocks to concentration.

CHAPTER 1: "WHY CAN'T I CONCENTRATE?"

> *"A problem well-stated is half solved."*—Charles Kettering

Having a problem with concentration doesn't mean you can't concentrate at all. It just means maybe you can't concentrate for *as long* as you would like to. Or you can't concentrate *when* you would like to. Maybe you have a problem *regaining* concentration after you've been interrupted or distracted.

The word "problem" doesn't necessarily need to have negative connotations. It simply means your *existing* situation (what you have) is not your *ideal* situation (what you want).

Keep Charles Kettering's advice in mind; your first step is to state *why* you have the problem. Some philosophers and scientists feel the word "why" is the most important word in the human language. Are you wondering why this is so? Doesn't that give you some insight into why it is?

The word "why" is responsible for much of our knowledge, understanding, motivation, and problem solving. That is why this book explores the "why's" of concentration *before* outlining the "how-to's." From this day forward, if you are not able to concentrate in a particular situation, just ask yourself "why?" Doing this will help you pinpoint and state the *source* of your problem, "I can't concentrate because..." and then you'll be half way to solving it.

WHY?

EXERCISE: BLOCKS TO CONCENTRATION

Think of some times when you've been unable to concentrate. Why couldn't you?
List blocks that kept you from concentrating as well as you would have liked.

1. _____

2. _____

3. _____

4. _____

5. _____

6. _____

7. _____

8. _____

9. _____

10. _____

ELEVEN BLOCKS TO CONCENTRATION

The following eleven items are the most common blocks to concentration. Use them as a checklist and see if any are relevant for you.

Block #1 *Distractions and interruptions.* Obviously, it's going to be tough to concentrate if you are being assaulted by noise, people, visual movement, and phones; all of which are competing for and dividing your attention.

Block #2 *Lack of training and/or practice.* Concentration is a skill. You can't expect to be good at it if you've never been taught how to do it, or if you don't have opportunities to use it on a daily basis.

(A quick note about this. Some older people grow concerned because they feel they're losing mental sharpness (e.g., they can't remember where they put things, they find it difficult to pay attention for any length of time.) Studies on the mind and aging have concluded that when senior citizens have a problem concentrating, it's usually not because they *can't* concentrate, it's because they *don't* concentrate. It's not that they have physical deterioration in brain function, it's that they are not regularly involved in activities that require mental effort or discipline. It's a question of the mind *rusting* out, not *wearing* out.

Block #3 *Habit of inattention/preoccupation.* Some people have so much going on in their lives, it is just normal for them to be ''scattered.'' Trying to do or think many things at once is the way they've always operated. In all likelihood, they adopted this style from the example set by their parents or friends and they've never had any reason to question it. Since we're creatures of habit, we tend to keep programmed patterns of behavior unless we have what's called an S.E.E. A **S**ignficant **E**motional **E**vent is a powerful insight that causes you to (figuratively) stop in your tracks and re-evaluate the way you're acting. This analysis often reveals a style that is working *against* you and not *for* you, and you're motivated to change your behavior for the better. (A classic S.E.E. is a life-threatening illness that prompts someone to change his/her eating and/or exercising habits.) We hope this book will serve as a *painless* S.E.E. for you. You'll become so convinced of the importance of concentration, that you'll work to counteract a lifetime of being perpetually preoccupied.

ELEVEN BLOCKS TO CONCENTRATION
(Continued)

Block #4 *Low frustration tolerance.*

> *"There are two kinds of people in this world, those who have learned to work through frustration, and those who wish they had."*—Anonymous

Much of today's society focuses on making your life as easy as possible (e.g., just count the number of commercials on TV that are designed to make your life convenient and free of hardship). That can be nice in terms of freeing you from time consuming menial labor, but it can make it tough to develop the mental discipline that's needed to concentrate on complex tasks.

This has particularly unwelcome significance for children. Many teachers have identified *Attention Deficit Disorder* as a major problem facing school children. Teachers feel lack of chores and responsibilities in the home, video games, and watching TV (which averages approximately 7¼ hours a day in American homes) all contribute to a generation that thrives on constant stimulation and immediate gratification. Many children are accustomed to fast-paced, action-packed TV shows with "instant" solutions and to switching the channel the second they get bored. It is difficult for teachers to compete with this. Classroom learning requires **mental patience** and **determination** (concentration), the antithesis of low frustration tolerance. Specific tips on how to help children develop concentration (the ability to stay on task) are presented later in this book.

Block #5 *Lack of interest or motivation.* Simply said, there is no concentration without interest. What this means is if you are working on a task that has no natural attraction for you, you must *arbitrarily* provide interest to motivate yourself, or else your mind will persist to resist!

Block #6 *Procrastination.* Procrastination is defined as the *automatic* postponement of an unpleasant task, *for no good reason.* Some people *habitually* put off unappealing matters without taking into account the consequences of their delay. Procrastination is a variation on the theme of low frustration tolerance; if the mind doesn't like what it's been told to do, it just says, "I'll do it later...."

Block #7 *Unclear purpose or plan.* David Campbell once said, "If you don't know where you're going, you'll probably end up somewhere else." Sometimes when you can't concentrate, it's because your mind was never given an order. Give your mind a destination (chosen project) and a mental road map (visualization), or step-by-step action plan. Perhaps you've heard the story about the disoriented pilot who radioed the control tower, "I may be lost; but I'm making record time!" Have you ever come to the end of the day and realized that you had been busy every minute, gotten a lot of things done, but they weren't very important things? An old saying is "all the mistakes I have made, all the errors I have committed, all the follies I have witnessed, have been the result of...*action without thought!*" Concentration is action *with* thought (and purpose). There is another reason that unclear purpose or planning blocks concentration. Anxiety can be defined in two words, "not knowing." If the mind doesn't know what it's supposed to do and how it's supposed to do it, it will be in a state of anxiety.

Block #8 *Mental clutter/overload.* For some people, an inability to concentrate isn't the result of their failure to choose a project, it's because they've chosen *too many!* If you have too many commitments, obligations, and deadlines clamoring for your attention, your mind just (figuratively) throws up its hands and says "I can't take it anymore!" Are you saying, "It would be impossible to choose one top priority, *they're all* important?" In Chapter 3, you'll learn how to concentrate even when it seems like everything has to be done right now...*first!*

Block #9 *Fatigue, stress, poor health.* Concentration is **directed mental energy**. If you're tired, physically out-of-shape, or sick, you simply won't have the energy necessary to apply yourself mentally. Drugs can chemically affect your ability to focus and hold attention. There is a famous story about a man who took Halcion (a sleeping pill) so he could get some rest on the plane. When he arrived at his destination, he couldn't remember why he had made the trip. Read the caution label on any medication you may be taking. If it warns against side effects of drowsiness or restlessness, this drug may be physically undermining your ability to concentrate. Check with your doctor for alternative medication.

ELEVEN BLOCKS TO CONCENTRATION
(Continued)

| Block #10 | *Unresolved emotions.* Sometimes when you aren't able to focus and maintain attention, it isn't because you *can't*, it's because another |

major problem is demanding all your attention and there's none left over for your other responsibilities.

Marilyn was worried because she seemed to have lost her ability to concentrate. When asked the most important question in the world, "Why? What was going on in her life that could be causing this problem?" she said that she was going through an unwanted divorce that involved a bitter child custody battle. No wonder she couldn't concentrate! Concentration is an *acquired* ability. If she had trained herself in this skill (if she had a Master's Degree in concentration), she might have been able to compartmentalize this painful event so she could function efficiently. Figuratively speaking though, she was still in concentration kindergarten. Her brain had a mind of its own and naturally dwelled on this disturbing, emotional trauma.

A simple and insightful exercise on page 80 can help determine if you might have unresolved problems that are blocking your ability to concentrate.

| Block #11 | *Negative attitude.* This is the most powerful block of all. Respected psychologist William James said, "We act in accordance with our |

beliefs." You can even have all the other elements going "right" for you, but if in your mind you don't believe you can concentrate, you will be right! If you say, "I can't concentrate in that crazy office," you'll be right! If you say, "I can't concentrate under pressure," you'll be right! This book will outline several methods you can use to talk yourself *into* concentrating as opposed to talking yourself *out of* even trying to mentally apply yourself.

The following parts in this book will show you how you can concentrate *despite* the clever obstacles presented in this section that try to block your efforts. These practical "how-to's" can enable you to focus and maintain your attention anytime, anywhere! Read on!

CHAPTER 2: "HOW CAN I LEARN THE SKILL OF CONCENTRATION?"

> *"To learn anything, we must first suspend disbelief."*—Anonymous

Some people believe they can't concentrate. They may even make claims like, "I'm so absent-minded. I'd forget my head if it wasn't attached." They are a victim of their own doubts. Shakespeare's King Lear made this wise observation: "Our doubts are traitors to us, for they rob us of the good we might achieve by attempting." It's true, isn't it? Maybe you know some people who has concluded they'll never be able to learn how to use a computer. By convincing themselves of this, they don't even try to learn it, and end up surrendering any chance they might have of benefiting from this valuable tool.

You *can* concentrate. Identifying a time when you have concentrated well can help you acknowledge that fact so you don't proceed with your "mental arms crossed."

EXERCISE

Have you ever been rushing to complete a project and hours went by without even being aware of them? Have you ever "played out of your head" or been "in the zone" when competing in a sport? Were you ever in a survival situation where you had to concentrate, or else? Have you ever been playing a game of checkers or chess and it seemed like nothing else existed except for the playing board? Describe a time you concentrated well and try to pinpoint *why* you were able to concentrate in that situation.

_____

_____

_____

_____

_____

LEARNING THE SKILL OF CONCENTRATION
(Continued)

You learn to concentrate as you would any other skill such as playing the piano. You start with the simplest fundamentals and practice them over and over until you can perform them *consistently and without thinking*. Next you combine these fundamentals and rehearse them in more complicated and demanding situations. Finally, you incorporate your newly learned fundamentals into ''real life'' situations. As with any skill, you must continue to practice. If you don't, you'll lose your ''touch.'' If you do, you'll maintain proficiency and continue to improve.

The five step exercise is your means to an end of acquiring the skill of concentration. This exercise teaches your mind to follow orders. It requires your mind to maintain focus on a chosen project. It gives you opportunities to practice *thought stoppage*. It helps you learn how to regain focus following a distraction. Mastering these fundamentals will then enable you to concentrate better in real-life situations. This exercise is the equivalent of practicing scales on the piano. The scales help you learn how to play the piano (notes, keys, finger placement and movement). After becoming proficient at that, you can play music.

EXERCISE: LEARNING THE SKILL OF CONCENTRATION

1. *Isolate yourself and remove all distractions.* Wait until the end of the day so you are finished with (and not distracted by) the day's obligations. Retire to a quiet room. Make sure you have privacy. Turn off the radio and TV. Sit in a not *too* comfortable chair in an upright and relaxed position.

2. *Select a simple assignment.* An assignment that has proven successful for hundreds of people is to either read, write, or say aloud for five minutes the four word phrase, **"I'm gooood at concentration."** Emphasizing "gooood" may not be grammatically correct, but it lends itself to being said with *fervor*, which is the point of this exercise. Repeating this phrase over and over has double value because it also works as an *affirmation*. An affirmation is a short, positive statement about ourselves that is phrased in the present tense. Your subconscious adopts affirmations as reality so positive self-talk can shape and improve your self image. By repeating **"I'm gooood at concentration,"** you'll be learning how to concentrate *and* you'll be developing a belief that you are talented at this skill.

People have preferred sensory styles. Some people love to read and can spend hours happily engaged in a good book. Other people can express themselves best when they put their thoughts down on paper. Some are verbal and enjoy talking with others. What is your preferred sensory style? If it is reading, then your assignment is to first write the words **"I'm gooood at concentration"** in large letters, and simply read them over and over again. If you like writing, then write the four word phrase over and over. If you enjoy speaking, then close your eyes (so you are not visually distracted), and repeat out loud with intensity **"I'm gooood at concentration. I'm gooood at concentration."**

3. *Set an alarm clock to go off in five minutes.* (You don't want to distract yourself by worrying about how much time has gone by.) *Give your mind its assignment,* "I'm going to read, write, or say **"I'm gooood at concentration"** and think about *only that* for five minutes. *Begin!*

> **Note:** Don't "try" to concentrate. "Trying" to do something (e.g., picking up a pencil) doesn't get the job done. You either pick up the pencil or you don't. Likewise, scrunching up your face, furrowing your brow, clenching your jaw, tensing up your neck and shoulders, and telling yourself to concentrate will not produce concentration! Simply *start* doing your assignment with all your attention and you *will* be concentrating.

EXERCISE (Continued)

4. *If you think of anything else, practice THOUGHT STOPPAGE and return to your original task with greater intensity.* This is a particularly important point. Who controls what is on your mind at any given time? You do! Yet isn't it true people say things like, ''I just can't stop thinking about...'' or ''I can't get my mind off...'' Recognize once and for all that you have the power to control what you think about. *Thought stoppage can be learned.* As soon as you become aware that you are thinking of something other than your chosen project, simply break off in mid-thought, say **''NO!''** and return to your original project with greater intensity. Read with exaggerated head movements, press down harder as you write, or speak more forcibly so your mind is fully occupied and less likely to wander.

Be patient and persistent. Getting upset, or scolding yourself for becoming distracted, is in itself a distraction. Telling yourself *not* to think about something means you're dwelling on the very thought you don't want to be thinking about! For example, if you say to yourself, ''This sure is a silly exercise,'' then get flustered ''Oh no, I'm not supposed to think about anything else,'' you are straying further from your chosen project. Instead, as soon as you become aware of the intruding thought, simply, say ''NO!'' and replace it with your original assignment (e.g., ''I wonder how much time has gone by...''NO!''...**''I'm gooood at concentration, I'm gooood at concentration''**).

Repeat this exercise every night. When you are able to maintain attention on your original task of reading, writing, or saying **''I'm gooood at concentration''** for five minutes without becoming distracted (this takes most people two to three weeks), *then start introducing distractions.* Turn on the radio; open your eyes if you are speaking out loud; sit in a room where there are other people. Repeat the exercise with distractions every night until you are able to concentrate for five minutes despite having things compete for your attention. This takes most people another two to three weeks (the length of time required to change an old habit or acquire a new habit). Once you are able to give your mind an order and have it obey despite distractions, you are ready to transfer these skills to the real world.

5. *Practice this exercise with everyday projects.* Instead of repeating **"I'm gooood at concentration,"** rehearse a report you are going to have to give at a staff meeting, or mentally prepare a list of things that need to be done the next day. The key point is to give your mind a specific order with a time deadline, and then to hold your mind to that assignment without allowing yourself to become distracted. A sample assignment might be, "I am going to prepare for tomorrow's job interview by anticipating what questions might be asked, and by composing answers that will help me win the job. I will think of that only for the next five minutes. "One reason why I am a good candidate for the job is because I'm a self starter. The ad mentioned you were looking for someone who doesn't need a lot of supervision (Oh no, what if Les is applying for the same job? He has more experience than I do…"NO!"… *"One reason is because I'm a self starter. This reference letter from my previous supervisor refers to a project I initiated and produced…).''*

Jim said, "I can't keep my mind 'on my mind' for this long." *EXACTLY!* Can you imagine what it would be like not to have the full use of your hands or your legs? Imagine how difficult it would be to function if you didn't have control of your body. Many people don't have the full use or control of their minds! Are you the master in your own "house" or are you a slave to your thoughts? Practicing this exercise for the next few weeks is one of the best investments you could ever make for yourself. It can put an end to "mind mutiny" and put you back in charge, where you belong!

Don't expect immediate results. There is no magic pill or formula that will give you instant concentration. Learning any skill takes time, and requires persevering through three levels of skill acquisition. Complete this next exercise to gain an insight into the three-stage process you go through to master a new skill.

SKILL ACQUISITION AHEAD

EXERCISE: SKILL ACQUISITION

What is one of your talents or skills? Are you an accomplished cook? Do you enjoy photography? Are you good at horseback riding or swimming?

In your best handwriting, write down in a short sentence something you're good at. For example, "I'm a good bowler," or "I'm a good carpenter," or "I'm a good bridge player."

_____

Now, write the same sentence *with your other hand.*

_____

How does that second sentence look? How did it feel to write it? Is handwriting a skill? Riding a bike? Using a typewriter? How about concentration? Sure, all of them are skills. You weren't born knowing how to do these things. You had to learn them step by step. Interestingly, there are three steps to acquiring a new skill and they all start with the letter A.

THE THREE "A's" OF SKILL ACQUISITION

1. Awkward

It's true, isn't it? When you first try something, you usually don't do it very well and it feels awkward. Remember the first time you rode a bicycle? Maybe you didn't go very far and your ride would have probably ended in a crash if someone wasn't there to support you. Instead of getting frustrated though and giving up ("I'll never do that again"), you were reassured that awkward performance is to be expected. It's the very natural first stage of learning. You wanted to be able to ride that bike, so you kept trying. Because you did, you progressed to the next stage:

2. Applied

At this stage, if you applied the techniques you learned, you got better results. In handwriting, you focused on how to shape your letters and you were able to write legibly. In swimming, if you remembered to keep your head down, breathe to the side, stroke your arms and kick your feet, you were able to stay afloat and get to the other side of the pool. If driving a car with a gear shift, you were able to get around a corner or accelerate from a stop sign without stalling the car. If you persisted through this stage, you arrived at that wonderful final stage which is:

3. Automatic

At this point, you didn't even have to think about what you were doing, it came naturally. Now, you could type the letters without even having to look at your fingers on the keyboard. In tennis, you didn't even have to think "racquet back, eyes on the ball, step into it, follow through." You just thought, "I'll hit this one cross-court."

What do the Three "A's" of Skill Acquisition have to do with concentration? When you start practicing your concentration skill-building exercise, it may feel awkward and you may not do it very well. Your mind may persist in wandering, or you may not be able to regain your train of thought after becoming distracted. Don't give up! You're just in the very natural first stage of skill acquisition. **If at first you don't succeed, you're about average.** This little exercise does work—if you do!

Still skeptical? Ask yourself if acquiring this important skill isn't worth an investment of five minutes a night for six weeks. Hundreds of people have found that practicing this exercise has enabled them to lengthen their attention span. They have developed the power to concentrate, despite distractions and disinterest. Perhaps most importantly, they have learned how to control their minds by mastering thought stoppage.

P A R T

II

Barriers To Concentration

CHAPTER 3: "WHAT IF I DON'T *FEEL* LIKE CONCENTRATING?"

Remember one block to concentration was "lack of motivation?" What if you have to concentrate on something that doesn't interest you? This chapter outlines suggestions for motivating yourself to concentrate and for *arbitrarily* providing interest so you can hold your attention on tasks—even when they're boring or tedious.

First, it's important to understand what motivates people. For people to be motivated to act, they must have a firm reason *why* this action will be worth their while. From the moment you wake up to the moment you go to sleep, there are only *two* reasons why you do anything. You do things because you *have* to, and you do things because you *want* to. Isn't it true if you do things because you have to, you do them with what are called the three R's. Can you guess what the three R's are?

What's something you don't like to do, but *have* to? Perhaps it's completing your income tax forms, writing a long budget proposal, or reading a dry, technical book. If you have to work on this unappealing task, you'll eventually concentrate on it, but with what? *Reluctance? Resistance? Resentment?* (A workshop participant once said, "If I have to do something I don't want to do, I'll do it...but with *revenge!*)

The point of this is *you won't concentrate if you feel you have to!* You need to get yourself into a "want to" frame of mind. How can you do this? By thoroughly convincing yourself of the enormous benefits of concentrating so you have firm reasons why you *want* to apply yourself.

Think about it. Doesn't your ability to concentrate affect almost everything you do? Becoming aware of concentration's many rewards, and understanding the significant role concentration plays in determining success can motivate you to *want* to concentrate because you will be convinced it will be worth your while. The next page lists just a few of the many advantages gained by concentrating well.

BENEFITS OF CONCENTRATION

1. *Output is increased.* You simply get more done when you are 100% attuned to your task. That means you get more letters written, papers corrected, projects completed, and goals achieved.

2. *You perform optimally.* It makes sense. If you are giving total attention to something, you have the greatest chance of doing your best work. If you are preoccupied, it will be difficult to excel since you're only partially applying yourself to your performance. Isaac Newton said "If I have ever made any valuable discoveries, it has been owing more to patient attention than to any other talent."

3. *Time invested in projects is decreased.* This is particularly important for tedious jobs. If you don't feel like doing something in the first place (e.g., paying bills) wouldn't you rather have it over in an hour instead of stretching it out to three hours? Giving full attention saves time initially because tasks will not take as long to complete. It also saves the time it would take to correct the mistakes and omissions that are a byproduct of inattention.

4. *Confidence is increased.* Ask any athlete about confidence, and they will tell you that confidence and concentration are inter-dependent; they are like the chicken and the egg. If you acquire the ability to concentrate on command, you will feel more confident because you trust that you will perform your best. This trust leads to added concentration because you are not distracted by doubts and anxieties. Also, as Chapter Five outlines, visualization (a positive form of concentration) gives you recent, frequent, successful practice which is the source of confidence.

5. *Tranquility and peace of mind are enhanced.* There is a story (probably apocryphal) of a man who travels the world searching for the meaning of life. One day he climbs a high mountain to a monastery to get the advice of a monk who is reputed to be the wisest man on earth. When asked for the secret to happiness, the monk replies simply, "*Do* whatever you're doing."

In other words, become totally immersed in whatever it is you are experiencing. Savor the taste of the food you're eating, marvel at the beautiful sounds of the music you're listening to, glory in the youthful exuberance and curiosity of a child. Have you heard the famous quote by Gertrude Stein about Oakland, California; "There's no 'there' there." That is true of some people. They are always "somewhere else." They may be with someone physically, but their minds are a million miles away thinking about this meeting, worrying about that errand, or trying to figure out what someone meant when they said this. As a result they often feel frazzled. Bhagavad Gita said, "For him who has no concentration, there is no tranquility." Concentration is a way to live fully in the moment. It can help you focus on and appreciate what you have.

6. *You can accomplish desired goals and transcend your abilities and circumstances.* In an article titled "How to Make Your Mind Behave," Frederick Robinson said, "The men who achieve important positions in life depend less upon their natural special aptitudes or inherited gifts, than on this *acquired ability* to fix the attention upon any specific problem and to hold the mind to that problem until they have seen it through."

It's as simple as this. What do you want in life? You will increase your chances of attaining it if you cultivate the characteristics of concentration. In his book, *Peak Performers,* Charles Garfield found that a sense of *mission* (clarity of purpose and determination to achieve their "chosen project") was a primary attribute of successful people. Identifying something you really care about and devoting yourself to that pursuit can add *zest* to your life and make it more meaningful.

The next time you don't feel like concentrating, remind yourself of the many benefits of concentration. This should provide you with enough incentive so you'll *want* to apply yourself mentally. The following seven tips can put you into a "want-to-concentrate" frame of mind.

SEVEN TIPS FOR MOTIVATING YOURSELF TO CONCENTRATE ON UNINTERESTING TASKS

TIP 1. *Use the Five Minute Plan to get yourself started.*

A useful observation by well-regarded human behavioral psychologist William James is "we are more likely to *act* ourselves into feeling, than we are to *feel* ourselves into acting." In other words, a good way to make yourself *feel* like doing something is to *start* it.

For example, do you owe anyone a letter? Are you waiting until you *feel* like writing that letter? Face it, that letter may never get written if you wait until you feel like doing it. If you just sat down and started writing that letter, wouldn't you be glad to finally be following up on your good intentions? When you think about it, writing a letter isn't so onerous, is it? Why then do people postpone (or not take action on) things they know they need to do?

Did you ever study the Law of Inertia and the Law of Momentum in science class at school? These laws state that a "still body tends to stay stationary," and a "body in motion tends to stay in motion."

You can counter the Law of Inertia and help yourself gain momentum by making it a habit to use the Five Minute Plan. The Five Minute Plan simply means the next time you're contemplating a task and you are not motivated, say "I don't feel like starting on this project, AND I'M GOING TO START IT ANYWAY." The "deal" you make with yourself is that at the end of five minutes, if you're still not interested, you can stop. Most of the time though, once you have gotten yourself out of inertia and into motion, you are so glad to finally be getting this task out of the way that you are motivated to continue.

One thing I've not been doing because I haven't *felt* like it is

_____

_____

I realize I may never *feel* like doing this, so I am going to help myself get started by

_____

_____

> **TIP 2.** *Always give yourself a starting time and an ending time when contemplating a task.*

"That which can be done at any time, rarely gets done at all." Sometimes when you're not concentrating on a project, it's because your mind wasn't given a deadline. "I really should get that report finished" is more of a half-hearted wish than it is an order to the mind to focus. If you say to your son, "Your room really needs to be cleaned," he feels no obligation to act because you have not given him a time limit. If instead you said, "You have five minutes to pick up your room...starting now," he will jump into action because he knows exactly what is expected of him. Likewise, if you want your mind to "get to work," you need to give it an explicit order, such as, "I'm going to start on those invoices at 9:00 and work on them until 10:30."

When you assign yourself a starting and ending time for a project, be sure to give yourself *less* time than you think you need. Why? Because of a phenomenon called Parkinson's Law. This law states that a task expands (or contracts) to the time allocated for it. Think back to your high school days. Did one of your teachers ever assign a term paper at the beginning of the school year that was due at the end of the semester? When did you start working on it? A week or two before the deadline? Teachers are now countering this widespread practice by assigning term papers two weeks before they're due. Yes, they get a lot of complaining from students that "there's not enough time," but they receive consistently higher quality papers. The teachers are actually helping students concentrate by giving them a sense of urgency. They can't afford to be distracted by irrelevant matters; they are "forced" to focus on their chosen project.

A task I have not started because I haven't given myself a starting time or an ending time is

_____

_____

_____

I'm going to give myself clarity and a sense of urgency by ordering myself to start it by (date, time)

STARTING TIME

ENDING TIME

_____

and finish it by

_____

MOTIVATING A GROUP TO CONCENTRATE ON UNINTERESTING TASKS

Have you ever chaired a meeting in which the participants seemed more interested in their weekend plans than in the items on your agenda?

Use a modification of Tip 2 when you chair meetings or facilitate planning retreats to keep the group on task.

Instead of asking for suggestions and running the risk of being met with dreaded silence, divide the group into brainstorming teams of four to five people, assign a specific task (''What are three things we can do to help make every customer a repeat customer?'' or ''Suggest five new slogans for our new advertising campaign'') and then give them a short time (ten to fifteen minutes) to produce ideas.

They may initially grumble about your being a strict ''taskmaster,'' but they will likely jump right into the task, discuss it animatedly, and produce innovative answers.

Ask each group to select a spokesperson to ''report back,'' and appoint someone to record contributions on large poster paper so you have a visual record everyone can see (and take pride in).

By getting all meeting participants actively involved in discussing and solving problems, you can set up *collective concentration* on group issues—one hallmark of a good team.

> **TIP 3.** *Use Henry Ford's wise advice. Divide and conquer.*

The man known as the Father of the Assembly Line once said, "Nothing is particularly difficult if you divide it up." Sometimes if you're finding it difficult to concentrate, it's because your chosen project is overwhelming. If your mind perceives that the order is impossible, it will balk. It doesn't want to attempt something that it "can't do." *It doesn't like to fail.*

Have you heard about the grueling Ironman Triathalon held in Kona, Hawaii every October? It starts with a 2.4 mile swim followed by a 100 mile bike ride, and finishes with a full marathon run. Therese decided she was going to compete in this challenging endurance race. After a couple of months, she became so discouraged by the enormity of preparing for such a demanding physical test that she quit training. A few weeks later she re-evaluated her decision and realized she had unnecessarily demoralized herself into giving up by thinking of the Ironman in its entirety. She decided to divide up her conditioning program. Instead of thinking about swimming, biking, and running the total distances, she just focused on achievable distances that posed a significant challenge for her. When she was able to swim a mile, bike 25 miles, and run 7 miles, she added more distance. Due to this graduated, one-step-at-a-time preparation, she was able to complete the race. Therese credits her success to her decision to concentrate on "possible" increments instead of on the whole "impossible" task.

Henry Ford's advice also helped me. I wanted to write a book for years, but as a mother, wife, and businesswoman, I had concluded there weren't enough blocks of time left over to be an author, too. Only after changing my beliefs did I finally undertake this project. What was my new approach? Instead of writing a book (an overwhelming prospect that boggled my mind), I wrote *chapters*. (Thank you, Mr. Ford!)

Is there something you've been putting off? Has it been because the task (anything from *house*work to *home*work) loomed too large in your mind? Can you divide it up so it's more palatable? I've been putting off

_____

_____

_____

I'm going to divide it up into achievable increments by

_____

so I feel capable of successfully attempting it.

SEVEN TIPS TO MOTIVATE YOURSELF TO CONCENTRATE (Continued)

> **TIP 4.** *If you're bored with a task...make it more difficult.*

A friend offered insight into why this works. He said, "No one ever gets bored eating tacos! You *have* to pay attention or you'll end up wearing them!" Likewise, if you're working on something that's not very stimulating...contrive to make it more demanding so you *have* to pay attention. If you're reading a dry, technical book, force yourself to pick up the pace. If you're in a meeting and your mind is taking a vacation, force yourself to sit up, lean forward, look at the speaker, and raise your eyebrows in an expression of interest. If you're playing tennis and you're spraying balls all over the court, force yourself to bend your knees and hit every return six feet over the net and deep into the opposing court. *Create* consequences so your mind doesn't have the luxury to be lazy.

A task I find boring is: _____

_____

I'm going to make it **demand** my attention by: _____

_____

_____

> **TIP 5.** *Fast-forward to the benefits and focus on them instead of on the difficulties.*

Have you seen Jack Nicklaus play golf recently? He looks pretty good, doesn't he? A reporter complimented Jack on his appearance and asked what he was doing to keep in shape. Jack replied, "I'm jogging." The reporter asked, "So, you really like to jog, huh?" Jack looked at him and said, "No, I hate it. But I like what it does for me!" This is a classic example of someone who has helped himself concentrate on something he'd never even do otherwise—by choosing to focus on why it will be worthwhile instead of why he doesn't like it. He instinctively understands a fundamental law of human behavior. In order to act, the perceived benefits must outweigh the perceived difficulties.

Wanda was suffering from the "empty nest syndrome." Her five children had all left home for lives of their own, and she had lots of time to fill for the first time in almost 30 years. She realized that something she had wanted to do ever since she left school for the birth of her first child, was to go back and finish college. She told her husband about her concerns (she'd be much older than the other students, she wasn't very excited about the thought of homework, it was going to be a hassle trying to track down her old school records). Her biggest concern was that it was going to take her three years to complete her studies. She said "I'll be almost 50 years old by then!" He wisely asked, "How old will you be in three years if you don't go back to school and get your degree?" He suggested she focus on how satisfying it would be to march up on stage to receive her diploma. He helped her vividly imagine what a boost it was going to give her self-esteem and how this would open up so many new doors. Wanda decided to focus on the benefits instead of the difficulties and now she has a bachelor's degree to show for it!

If you find yourself hesitating to take action on something because of doubts or laziness, ask yourself, **"What will matter a year from now?"** Many individuals trying to get in shape promise themselves they're going to get up at dawn and go for a swim. What often happens is their alarm gives off at the rude hour of 6:00 A.M. and they ask themselves, "Whose idea was this, anyway?" It's very tempting at that point just to roll over and dive under the pillow. They can counter this temptation by asking, "Will it matter a year from now that I got an extra hour of sleep? Or will it matter more that I have taken a positive step toward improving myself?"

TIP 5. *Fast-forward to the benefits...(Continued)*

In an article on "Happiness," an interviewer asked dozens of people one question, "What has made you happy?" The final paragraph had the answer of an eighty year old man. "When I think back over my life, I realize that I don't regret a single thing I've done. *I only regret the things I didn't do!*"

Did you see the movie *Cabaret*? In the theme song, Sally Bowles (Liza Minelli) belts out the rhetorical question *"What good is sitting alone in your room?"* The next time you're not concentrating (starting) on something that would enrich your life, ask yourself these questions, "What will matter a year from now? What good is sitting alone in my room? Am I leading a life that will lead to regrets?" Hopefully, this will give you the incentive to take action (concentrate) on a chosen project that will add value to your life.

Something I've not done because I've been focusing on the difficulties instead of the benefits, is

_____

_____

_____

_____

_____

_____

_____

_____

I'm going to choose to fast forward to the benefits. I'm going to focus on

_____

_____

_____

_____

_____

_____

to move myself into action.

TIP 6. *Verbally minimize an unpleasant task.*

Have you ever been looking for something in your refrigerator, noticed some out-of-date yogurt hiding on a back shelf, and said to yourself, "I really should throw that away"—and then closed the door and went about your business? Sometimes the things you're not concentrating on would only take seconds or minutes to do. The next time you're about to mindlessly pass over something that needs to be done, ask yourself how long it will take. If it's only a minute, SAY SO. Saying out loud "I'm here; this will only take two minutes" makes it almost embarrassing not to attend to the task at-hand.

What's a task you have to do frequently that you don't like to do? (Maybe it's filling out a time card or a mileage record, or setting up the lawn sprinklers, or going to the post office).

_____

_____

_____

How long does it take? From now on, I'm going to motivate myself to do this without grumbling by saying

_____

_____

_____

SEVEN TIPS TO MOTIVATE YOURSELF TO CONCENTRATE (Continued)

TIP 7. *Self-talk yourself out of procrastination.*

One definition of procrastination is the "automatic postponement of an unpleasant task—*for no good reason.*" The key word is "automatic" (without considering the consequences, you just think "I'll do it later").

Is your motto "Procrastinate now?" Have you ever driven past a gas station, looked at your car's gas gauge, seen that it's almost empty, and thought "I'll get it tomorrow"? The following self-talk approach can help reverse this habit.

What is something on which you've been procrastinating? (This could be paying bills, organizing pictures in the family photo album, or making a dental appointment.)

_____

_____

Ask yourself these questions to bring you face to face with the consequences of delaying action.

Do **I have** to do this task? _____

If the answer is no, then this isn't procrastination. You may be putting this off, but with good reason. Maybe you've postponed doing the housework. It has to be done, but do *you* have to do it? If you really dislike it, would it be worth $50 a week to pay someone else to do it so you can have time for higher priority items?

Ted had a real insight when he asked himself "Do **I have** to do this?" His TV was broken and weeks had gone by and he hadn't taken it in to be fixed. He recognized he didn't *have* to get the television fixed. In the past few weeks, he read more books and spent more time with friends than he had for years. He decided his life was better without TV.

If your answer is "Yes, **I** do **have** to do this task," then move on to the next question.

Do I **want** to have this task **done**? _____

Is the answer "No"? Then once again, you're delaying action, but perhaps with good reason. A couple used to buy houses, live in them while they remodeled them, sell them for a profit, and then move to a new house and start the process all over again. They were upset with themselves because they kept putting off the final touches needed to get one house ready to put on the market. When they asked themselves these questions, they realized the truth was they enjoyed living in that particular neighborhood. They had tired of their nomadic lifestyle and didn't want to uproot themselves all over again. Talking through this situation helped them see that they weren't being "lazy," they were just ready to settle down.

Is your answer "Yes, I do **want** to have this **done**?" Then move on to the next question.

Will this task be any **easier** to do **later**? _____

If the answer is "Yes," then once again, you're putting it off—but with good reason. A young man had been given a project that required advanced computer skills. The problem was, he was still learning how to use the system. Even though he only had until Friday to complete the project, he decided it would be beneficial to wait until Wednesday to start. Why? Because the office computer-whiz had several hours available that day and with his help the project would be completed in half the time.

If your answer is "No, this task won't be easier to do later"—THEN DO IT NOW!

This is the "Face the Music" approach to procrastination. If you have to do it, if you want to have it done, and if you realize it won't be any easier later, then start it now. Thomas Huxley said, "One of the toughest things to learn is the ability to make yourself do the thing you have to do, when it ought to be done, whether you like it or not; it is the first lesson that ought to be learned; and however early a man's training begins, it is probably the last lesson that he learns thoroughly."

Be sure to ask yourself these three questions whenever you don't feel like concentrating on something. (e.g., you're working through your in-basket and every time you get to a less-than-appealing task you put it on the bottom of the stack and say to yourself "I'll do that one later.")

TALK YOURSELF OUT OF PROCRASTINATION (Continued)

From now on I'm going to self-talk myself out of procrastinating on

_____

_____

_____

_____

_____

_____

by _____

_____

_____

_____

Are you wondering why a book on concentration spends so much time discussing procrastination? Because a mental ''mañana'' attitude precludes concentration—it doesn't give it a chance. The techniques discussed in this chapter can help you reverse a habit of procrastination by learning how to *arbitrarily provide interest* in unpleasant tasks you'd otherwise postpone. In short, you now know how to motivate yourself to concentrate—even when you don't feel like it.

CHAPTER 4: "HOW CAN I CONCENTRATE DESPITE DISTRACTIONS?"

Many people feel distractions and interruptions are their biggest deterrent to concentration. Fortunately, many distractions can be eliminated or reduced. Complete the following questionnaire to gain some insight into whether your office setting is supporting or undermining your work efforts. If you are a student, a home-based entrepreneur, or a homemaker, then think of a place at home where you try to study, conduct business or pay bills.

WORK ENVIRONMENT EVALUATION

	YES	SOMETIMES	NO
1. Do you have a private office (workplace) with a door you can close for privacy?	☐	☐	☐
2. Does your desk face the wall so you are not visually distracted by foot traffic and/or the activities of others?	☐	☐	☐
3. Does your phone ring more than 20 times a day?	☐	☐	☐
4. Are you responsible for responding to customers and/or visitors more than ten times a workday?	☐	☐	☐
5. Are you interrupted by in-person visits from others more than ten times a day?	☐	☐	☐
6. Does the noise level in your office (copier, phones, computers, FAX) bother you?	☐	☐	☐
7. Are your work surroundings pleasing and comfortable (room is neat, chairs are comfortable, lighting is adequate).	☐	☐	☐
8. Are 75% or more of the materials you need daily within an arm's reach of your desk?	☐	☐	☐
9. Are file cabinets organized to the point you can retrieve needed files within one minute?	☐	☐	☐
10. Do you have stacks of UPO's (unidentified piled objects) on your desk?	☐	☐	☐

- For questions #1, 2, 7, 8 and 9, score five points for a yes answer, three points for a sometimes answer, and one point for a no answer.
- For questions #3, 4, 5, 6, 10, score one point for a yes answer, three points for a sometimes answer, and five points for a no answer.
- If your score totals up to 40 or more, good for you! Your environment is setting you up for success. If your score total is between 25 and 39, then you can help yourself by organizing your workplace so it's more conducive to concentration. If your score is 24 or less, no wonder you can't concentrate. Read this chapter twice, take action on the suggestions, and see if they don't make a significant difference for you.

THINGS YOU CAN DO TO CONCENTRATE BETTER

THING 1. CLEAN OFF YOUR DESK. Sure you've heard this before, but do you know why it's so important? Your attention is where your eyes are. If your desk is covered with phone messages, letters to be proofed and paperwork to be finished, then every time your eyes move even a fraction of an inch, you're distracted. Instead of focusing on the project in front of you, you're looking at that pink message slip and wondering what Joe wants to talk to you about, or you're looking at that budget report and worrying when you're going to have time to finish it. Realize how many times a day this happens, and you can see how important it is to make your desk a *work* place and not a *storage* place. A good rule of thumb is if you're not going to use (or work on) something that day, *it doesn't need to be on your desk.* One supervisor said, "I like a messy desk. I'm not a slob, I'm just organizationally challenged!" If you have an aversion to cleaning off your desk, at least help yourself concentrate on an important project by moving irrelevant papers aside (ideally behind you) so you won't be visually tempted. The old saying "out of sight, out of mind" has *literal* significance for concentration.

THING 2. DIPLOMATICALLY DEFLECT DROP-IN VISITORS.

It's important to be accessible to fellow employees, but at what cost? Dave said he wasn't getting any work done because he had become the "sympathetic ear" to everyone in the office. He didn't want to be rude, so even when co-workers kept him from working on an important project, he suffered in silence and later would need to come in early, work through lunch, or stay late to make up for these unpaid counseling sessions. He finally solved his problem (without offending his fellow workers) by taking the following steps:

a) He turned his desk so it faced a side wall and half-closed his office door. Dave's desk used to face the hallway and he was often distracted by people passing by. He'd look up from his work to see who it was, the person walking by would look in to see what he was doing, their eyes would meet and at that point it seemed downright unfriendly to look away. The person would say, "hello," step into his office, and they'd end up talking for several minutes. He realized this was happening ten to fifteen times a day. Even if each visit only took a couple of minutes, it really added up! Now, with his desk facing away from the corridor, he's not even aware of the foot traffic. By being pro-active, he has *prevented* interruptions. When people pass by, they see he's involved with work and they just keep walking unless they really need to talk with him. Dave said, "This simple change has made such a dramatic difference in my ability to concentrate at work!"

b) Dave established open-door hours from 9:00 to 11:00 in the morning and from 2:00 until 4:00 in the afternoon. If co-workers have suggestions, need his input, or want to voice grievances, they're welcome to come in and see him **during those hours only**. His employees have access to him, but on balanced terms. He has been able to get significantly more done because he has longer blocks of uninterrupted time for concentrated work. A beneficial by-product of this policy is that his employees have become more self-sufficient. In the past, if something went wrong, they just automatically came to him for advice. They became dependent on his guidance. Dave's new "partial" open-door policy encourages them to take responsibility for solving their own problems.

THINGS YOU CAN DO TO CONCENTRATE BETTER (Continued)

THING 2. DIPLOMATICALLY DEFLECT DROP-IN VISITORS (Continued)

c) If Dave is busy, he no longer hopes/assumes a visitor will be sensitive to the fact that this may not be a good time to interrupt him. Instead of sending subtle signals (tapping his pencil impatiently or pointedly looking at his watch), he speaks up and diplomatically deflects the discussion. By using the following tips on positive phrasing, he's found co-workers respond favorably to his request for postponement instead of feeling shunted aside.

- He starts off with their name. (It's the best way to make sure he has their attention.)

- He says "Jane, I *want* to discuss this with you" or "Bob, I know this is important." Notice he doesn't use negative words like "I can't talk to you, I'm busy" or "I don't have time to discuss this right now."

- He continues with "...*and* I need to get this agenda finished for our 10:00 meeting" or "...*and* I've got to get this in the mail by noon." Notice he used the words "and" instead of "but." The word "but" sets people up as adversaries and negates what's been said.

- He continues with "*Can we* get together after the meeting?" or "Can this wait until after I get this contract in the mail?" Notice instead of ordering, "This is just going to have to wait until..." or complaining "I've just got too much to do right now," he's asking.

- He closes with appreciation. "*Thanks*, Karen for understanding" or "I really appreciate your cooperation on this" or "I'll look forward to talking with you after lunch."

Dave was initially concerned that he might offend people with his new policies. Much to his relief and pleasant surprise, co-workers have told him they admire his courage in enforcing his priorities and have asked if he could teach them how to do it.

THING 3. MAKE YOUR PHONE A TOOL RATHER THAN A TYRANT.

TYRANT. Understand that just because someone calls doesn't mean you ought to automatically drop everything to deal with them. You may have to answer the phone, but once you find out the purpose of the call, determine whether it really should take precedence over your ''chosen project.'' Ask yourself, ''Is this call more important than what I am doing?'' If it is, by all means, handle it *after* you do something to facilitate your return to your original project. Wouldn't you agree that one of the frustrations of working around other people is being interrupted just as you've really gained momentum? Sometimes when you come back to what you were doing, you can't even remember what you were going to say. From now on, if you're interrupted while writing, jot down a key word of what you were going to write next *before* you switch your attention. If you're reading, underline the last sentence you read. If you're in the middle of a conversation, write down a few key words that capture the essence of what was being discussed. The few seconds this takes will save you hours of frustration by enabling you to quickly pick up your original train of thought instead of wondering, ''Where was I going with this?''

If the call is *not* more important than what you are doing, then use positive phrasing to diplomatically postpone the discussion. If a friend calls to set up plans for the weekend and you have an appointment in five minutes, say, ''Ross, I'm looking forward to our weekend *and* I need to get ready for an appointment in five minutes. Can I call you back this evening and we'll talk about it then? Thanks for understanding.''

What if a client has been talking non-stop for thirty minutes and you're thinking, ''I've got to get back to that proposal! I'm supposed to turn it in by 3:00!'' Don't suffer in silence and wait for them to bring the conversation to a close. Some people don't know when or how to stop talking. Sometimes people are lonely or they love having an audience. At work, you don't usually have the time to indulge these people (even if you'd like to), yet you certainly don't want to be abrupt and risk losing their friendship, business and good will.

THING 3. MAKE YOUR PHONE A TOOL RATHER THAN A TYRANT. (Continued)

When is it appropriate to interrupt someone and terminate a conversation? Visualize an old-fashioned scale. Your client or co-worker's needs are on one side of the scale, and you and your organization's needs are on the other side. Your goal is to try to keep the scale of needs in balance. If you have been listening to someone for thirty minutes (and their business is finished or they are just repeating themselves), then their needs have been met. What about your needs or the organization's needs? What if two other customers have been waiting to be served? At this point, it is appropriate and fair (not rude) to diplomatically interrupt the caller in an effort to get the scale of needs back in balance.

The following steps can help you *courteously control* the conversation and move to terminate the call without alienating the other person.

- *Say their name firmly and warmly.* Most people pause momentarily when they hear their name. That is your opportunity to get your ''verbal foot in the door.''

- *Summarize their comments.* Paraphrasing back what they've just said is the key to not upsetting someone. Repeating back their points assures them you really have been listening, and they won't resent your grabbing the conversational ball because they feel ''heard.''

- *Tell them what action you're going to take.* Use the magic words, *''As soon as I hang up, I'm going to. . .''* This phrase moves the conversation forward to the future (what's going to happen next) and finishes the conversation by putting it in the past.

- *Close in a firm and friendly way.* Inject courteous phrases such as ''Thank you for bringing this to my attention,'' or ''I'm glad we had a chance to talk'' to soften the impact of terminating the call. Your voice inflection needs to go down so there's a feeling of finality. An upward inflection implies you're asking for a response and they would be likely to start the conversation all over again. ''I'll look forward to. . .'' with your voice dropping on the last word is a polite way to close a discussion.

An example of how to courteously control a phone conversation so you can get back to concentrating on your chosen project is: ''Mr. Jones, I understand you requested this material last week and that you still haven't received it. As soon as I hang up, I'm going to personally put the information together and put it in the mail. I'm certainly sorry this happened, and I'm glad you called to tell me about it. You should have it by Monday. Thank you again for calling.''

Batching your calls (accumulating return calls and outgoing calls instead of making them on a piecemeal basis) *and establishing phone hours* (asking that people call only during specific hours) will free-up time so you can attain quality concentration and get more done because you're not being constantly interrupted by phone calls.

THING 4. KEEP A MASTER LIST OF ALL COMMITMENTS.

Do you use your mind as a mental bulletin board? When you think of something that needs to be done, do you say ''I've got to remember to call Joe about that conference'' or ''Oops, I can't forget to stop off at the dry cleaners on the way home.'' You are giving your mind **orders.** It obeys and ends up being a mental switchboard. Every five minutes or so it pipes up, ''Don't forget to call Joe,'' ''Remember to stop at the dry cleaners.'' Imagine how many times a day you give yourself mental messages and you can see why it's tough to concentrate! Get those memos out of your mind and write them down so you can ''free your mind.''

---

*Note: A 1989 study done by Priority Management reports that we spend *almost a year of our lives searching for lost items.* As one employee said, ''I can't remember where I put my reminder notes!'' Write down all your obligations on a master list. You'll greatly reduce your ''tracking down'' time if you only have one source.

THING 5. USE THIS THREE STEP GTD (Get Things Done) PLAN TO CONCENTRATE WHEN HANDLING MULTIPLE PRIORITIES.

Step 1. *Pick from your master list the seven most important tasks to be done that day.* You may be thinking, ''But I've got more things to do than that.'' Why only seven items?

- Most people can only maintain a maximum of seven items in their short term memory.

- A short list allows for the insertion and handling of those spontaneous matters and emergencies that crop up throughout the day that have to take precedence over what you're working on.

- Research has concluded that visual order can enhance mental order. In other words, if your ''to do'' list is a mish-mash of notes, you'll become confused everytime you look at it. If it neatly reflects what has to be done that day, your mind will have clear, organized ''marching orders.''

- How many items do you have on your ''to do'' list? Ten? Twenty? Thirty? One definition of stress is ''feeling overwhelmed.'' Does looking at your list prompt thoughts like ''I'll never be able to get through all that!'' Have you ever stopped to realize that you may be stressing yourself out just by looking at your ''to do'' list? Every glimpse leads to a feeling of being ''over-burdened''—and your mental load weighs down your energy. Keep your master list accessible, but out of sight (hence out of mind).

THING 5. USE THIS THREE STEP GTD (Get Things Done) PLAN TO CONCENTRATE WHEN HANDLING MULTIPLE PRIORITIES. (Continued)

- Are any of the items on your current "to do" list things you don't have to work on today? Then why are they on your list? Aren't they irrelevant matters? Why are you spending time today concentrating on items that really don't need to be attended to until next week? Keep your focus on your "chosen projects" (the items that should be done today) by getting out of your sight any mention of those irrelevant matters (things that don't have to be completed until later).

Step 2. *Now, on a fresh piece of paper, start at the top and list the seven items in order of priority.* Number one is the most pressing thing that needs to be done, number two is the second most important, and so on. Are you saying, "There's no way I could select just one thing that's *most* important. They're *all* important?"

It's important to understand a fundamental concept of concentration. *Your mind can only think of one thing at a time.* It can switch back and forth very quickly between several objects, but it is physically capable of holding only one thought at a time.

It may be true you have several projects that are all top priority. You still need to pick one that you're going to give your attention to right now. How can you decide which to tackle first? Ask, "What is the *primary* function of my job?" Instead of comparing tasks to each other (asking "Should I do this or that first?" will only lead to more confusion), compare them to your job **purpose.** Which of the tasks is most closely allied to that purpose? Which would help achieve it best?" This process can help you arrive at a one, two, three order and clarify your chosen project so you'll know what to concentrate on first.

This concept can be applied in all day-to-day activities and business matters. A small businessman reported, "I learned that lesson the hard way. I started off just offering printing services. Clients kept requesting assistance in other areas so I added on "help-yourself" copy machines, graphic design consulting, free delivery, and a variety of other services. I ended up almost going bankrupt! Not only was I running myself ragged, we weren't doing any of our jobs well anymore. We were the original 'jack of all trades, master of none.' I took a long hard look at my business and asked myself, "What do I enjoy most and what makes the most money? The answer to that was running a *quality* printing house. I got rid of all those other 'distractions' and started concentrating on what we did best. We're a healthy company again thanks to that decision."

Alexander Graham Bell said, ''The sun's rays do not burn until brought to a focus.'' Examine your life. What is your purpose? What are the five most important things in your life? What do you spend the most time on? What are you concentrating on in your life? As Harold Kushner so wisely said, ''No one ever said on their deathbed 'I wish I'd spend more time at work.''' Determine to live wisely by not frittering away your life on superfluous, less meaningful activities. Instead, concentrate on what you love and do best. To the degree possible, focus on your real priorities so you can live ''on purpose.''

Step 3. *Now, start working on your number one priority and work on it until you have it finished, until you need a break, or until a higher priority takes precedence.* In the *real* world, you may only get to concentrate on your top priority for a few minutes before you're interrupted. Use the techniques below to stay in charge of your work environment.

- Determine what the caller/visitor wants and ask yourself, ''Is this more important than what I'm working on right now?''

- If it is, switch your attention to it AFTER doing something to facilitate your return to your original project.

- If it is not, have the courage to diplomatically deflect or to courteously terminate the conversation so you can return to your top priority.

People who use the three step GTD plan claim it makes a real difference. Now, even when they're inundated with distractions, they have a system for determining what is important and what should be attended to first. You may be saying, ''I can see where this would work for people who work for themselves, but I report to someone else and he controls my workday, not me.'' Maybe you work for several bosses, and they interrupt you throughout the day to give you (sometimes conflicting) tasks. You need to control this if you are going to be optimally effective.

a) First, ask your boss(es) to help you decide what ''chosen projects'' need to be worked on first, and what (if anything) takes precedence on this list.

b) Establish a system to *accumulate* messages instead of having them interrupt you as they occur.

PICK THE MOST IMPORTANT TASKS

c) If you work for several bosses, and they give you conflicting orders, *don't make the decision yourself as to what to do first*. Don't proceed unless you have clarity about your chosen project. You don't want to make an ''executive decision'' and then find out after hours of hard work that it was the wrong one. Ask them which project you should concentrate on first.

You may be thinking, ''These techniques would help if I worked with *reasonable* people. Some employees are so pushy they'd just barge in anyway. They don't care if I'm trying to concentrate. They just want what they want!''

If you have to deal with ''bully'' personalities, ask yourself how long you're going to be a victim. Passively enduring insensitive demands may mean you miss deadlines, put in longer hours, and put strains on relationships. It's not necessary to turn aggressive and think only of *your* needs. Neither should you always put others' needs in front of yours. Concentration is having the courage to impose on time, people, and events your decision as to what's important; what must come first. Instead of mindlessly reacting to others' demands, balance them with your needs so you can get work done on a priority basis instead of just responding to whomever happens to walk into your office or call on the phone.

If you're thinking these are just common sense time management techniques, you're right! Isn't it true though that just because something is common *sense* doesn't mean it's common *practice!* **Practice** these techniques and you can take charge of your concentration and optimize your effectiveness.

EXERCISE: THINGS YOU CAN DO TO CONCENTRATE BETTER

a) A person who frequently breaks my concentration by coming in with requests or questions is

_____

_____

_____

_____

The next time this person interrupts me and I determine the situation is *not* more important than what I was working on, I'm going to

_____

_____

_____

_____

b) The next time I'm on the phone and the person on the other end of the line won't stop talking, I'm going to

_____

_____

_____

_____

c) I'm going to ask my boss to help me concentrate (so I can get more work done for him) by

_____

_____

_____

_____

d) I am going to reduce confusion and give myself some visual *and* mental order by

_____

_____

_____

_____

III

What Concentration Can Do For Me

· CAN DO ·

CHAPTER 5: "HOW CAN I USE CONCENTRATION TO BE MORE CONFIDENT?"

Visualization (vividly imagining exactly how you want to do something) is the single best thing you can do to improve your performance—in anything.

That's a pretty sweeping statement, isn't it? It's usually not wise to make such a broad generalization because it might invite readers to think of an exception that would disprove it. However, this statement can be backed up with evidence. Following are four reasons why visualization (a **positive** form of concentration) is perhaps the best thing you can do to improve your performance in anything you do.

WHY VISUALIZATION WORKS

1. *The mind doesn't differentiate between what's real and what's imagined.* Sound incredible? It's true. If you vividly imagine doing something, it's being recorded in your mind as if it were actually happening.

2. *Confidence is a result of recent, frequent, successful practice.* Wouldn't you agree that if you do something well, you've done it a lot, and you've done it recently, you will be able to walk into that situation with confidence?

3. *Nervousness is caused by focusing on your doubts and fears.* This is true, too, isn't it? Anxiety is a by-product of thinking about what could go wrong ("Oh no, I know I am going to blow it!"), and dwelling on worries and concerns ("What if they ask me why I was let go?").

4. *People are initially uncomfortable in unfamiliar surroundings.* You've probably heard of the "fight or flight" reflex. In potentially dangerous situations your body prepares you with adrenalin in case you need to defend yourself or flee.

Add these four statements together and what do you get?

- VISUALIZATION gives you recent, frequent, successful practice which gives you confidence.

- VISUALIZATION reduces nervousness because you're not thinking about your doubts and fears (you're thinking about what you *want* to do instead of what you *don't want* to do).

- VISUALIZATION optimizes performance by familiarizing you with your environment so it is not as distracting.

WHY VISUALIZATION WORKS (Continued)

Visualization **is a form** of concentration. Picturing in your mind exactly how you want to do something is another way to focus on your chosen project. Filling your mind with how you want to perform is giving your mind an order so it has a clear purpose.

There is another reason why visualization is so powerful. Visualization (*mental* practice) can be better than *actual "real-life"* practice. How so? You may be familiar with a study with a group of school boys. Half were put in a room and told to close their eyes and to practice shooting free throws in their mind. The other half went to the basketball court, were given balls, and given opportunities to practice free throws. After a half hour of practice, both groups were given ten free throws. Guess which group always scored highest? The group that had practiced in their minds. Because they had practiced "perfectly." Visualization was more effective. The boys on the court were missing most of their shots and their repeated errors were being imprinted.

For several years, this author had the privilege of working with Rod Laver, a famous tennis player who won the Grand Slam of Tennis twice. "Rocket" was known for his mental and physical fitness gained from hundreds of hours of on and off court drills. He said he didn't like the statement "practice makes perfect" because "No one can ever be perfect." He maintained instead that "practice makes *better*." He felt the *more* you practiced, the better you got, but more importantly, the *better* your practiced, would make you even better. Incredible as it seems, *visualizing exactly how you want to perform can often be more beneficial than "real-life" practice*. It's a way to practice "better."

Chinese pianist Liu Shih-Kun, winner of the second prize at the 1958 International Tchaikovsky Competition, was put in solitary confinement during the so-called Cultural Revolution. Shortly after being released, he performed with the Philadelphia Orchestra in Peking. An audience member approached him after the performance to marvel at the quality of his playing. He remarked, "You're playing better than before! How can this be when you haven't touched a piano for six years?" Liu Shih-Kun calmly looked at him and replied "I played every day!"

What's an upcoming situation in which you'd like to be more confident? Are you planning to apply for a new position and you'd like to project poise during the job interview? Are you going to approach your boss to negotiate a raise? Are you going to a class reunion? Never attempt any kind of performance without first investing at least five to ten minutes in mental practice. Lackluster performance ("I'm having a lousy day," "This is a waste of time") is often due to the fact the mind was never given a specific goal or "warmed up." Every single time you embark upon an activity, be sure to first engage your mental gears by giving yourself a clear destination (purpose) and a mental road map (visualization).

MAKING VISUALIZATION A POSITIVE FORM OF CONCENTRATION

"Where the attention goes, the energy flows." —Zig Ziglar

Our thoughts turn into self-fulfilling prophecies. Put your mind to work *for* you by using the following four guidelines to make visualization a *positive* form of concentration.

Guideline 1. To the degree possible, picture where you'll be *in detail*. Are you going to be in your boss' office when you ask for that salary increase? Picture exactly what it will look like. What kind of chair will you be sitting in? What kind of desk does she have? Will the phone be ringing? Will people be coming in and out?

Guideline 2. Conjure up as many senses as possible for your mind picture. Are you going to be playing a concert in an outdoor amphitheater? Prepare yourself for the blinding effect of the stage lights. Imagine a cool, evening breeze ruffling the sheet music on your stand. Mentally accustom yourself to playing with street noise in the background. Have a "dress rehearsal" right in your mind so it's just like doing "the real thing."

Guideline 3. Visualize "chronologically" (from beginning to end) exactly how you want to perform in this situation. Mental practice has diminished value if you jump around from scene to scene. If you're mentally rehearsing for a round of golf, get a copy of the course layout and familiarize yourself with the layout of each hole. Imagine yourself walking up the first tee, picture yourself driving straight down the fairway, see yourself taking slow backswings with your irons, visualize keeping your head down on your putts.

Guideline 4. Picture *what you don't want, and plan what you're going to do if your worst nightmare happens.* You may be saying, ''Isn't that a contradiction? Wouldn't that make me nervous because I'd be focusing on my doubts and fears? It would if you only dwelled on your worries. Take it a step further. Determine in advance how you want to handle an unwanted situation, and then if it occurs, it will help you ''keep your cool'' (i.e. confidence and concentration) if it occurs. Great comedians are masters at this. They *plan* what they're going to do if a joke falls flat. When it happens, good comedians are ready with a rejoinder that is often funnier than the original one-liner. Politicians wouldn't dream of going into a press conference without having a staff member play ''devil's advocate'' and asking tough questions. By anticipating and preparing for controversial questions, they are reducing the risk of being unnerved when asked about a sensitive issue. Since real-life events may not unfold as you've ''scripted'' them in your visualization, expect the ''unexpected.'' Visualize how you would handle your boss saying ''We don't have money in our budget right now for the project you are working on.'' Think in advance how to respond if your boss asks you something you don't know, or asks if you want to work on an assignment that does not appeal.

If there was space, dozens of success stories could be related of others who got great results from visualization. On the following pages are two favorites because they demonstrate how using visualization to concentrate on what you want (instead of dwelling on what you fear) can help you overcome nervousness while setting up peak performance.

VISUALIZATION SUCCESS STORIES AHEAD

KEEP VISUALIZATION POSITIVE (Continued)

CASE #1—KIM

Kim confessed she was "scared to death" because she had been asked to speak at the national PSI (Professional Secretaries International) convention. She said, "There are going to be over 500 people in the audience, and I've never spoken to a group of more than five people in my life! Even though I know my topic cold and have been practicing for weeks, I can't sleep at night because I'm so worried about getting up in front of all those people. What if I forget what I'm supposed to say? What can I do?"

When asked when and where the convention was to be held she said, "In two weeks at the Coral Ballroom of the Hilton." The advice given to her was, "For the next couple of weeks, go to your room at the end of the day and sit in an upright but comfortable chair. Picture in your mind what the ballroom looks like and where you'll be sitting when you're introduced. See yourself standing up with dignity and walking *tall* to the podium. Imagine making warm eye contact with people in the different quarters of the room. Imagine yourself pausing until it's completely quiet and you have everyone's attention. Picture yourself smiling, welcoming them, and then saying your first few sentences, slowly, in a strong, distinctive voice that everyone can hear clearly. See yourself reaching out to your listeners and making your points in an organized and interesting way. See yourself closing with impact and graciously accepting the audience's applause. Picture this over and over again in your mind for ten minutes every night for the next two weeks."

She called the day after the conference and said, "It worked! I couldn't believe how confident I felt. It was like I had done it a hundred times before!" She *had* done it a hundred times before...in her mind!

CASE #2—MARTHA

Martha admitted that she was dreading her son's wedding. When asked, "Don't you like the bride?" she explained that she loved the bride, it was just that the bride was the only daughter of a very prominent family in town. She said, "I'm basically very shy and her parents seem so sophisticated and worldly. I was very uncomfortable during the engagement dinner because I just didn't know what to say. We're going to be seated next to each other at the reception, and I have no idea what we can talk about."

It was suggested that Martha use visualization to concentrate on the positive aspects of her son's wedding. "For the next few weeks, before you go to sleep, just picture yourself in the church. See your son standing at the altar and think back to when he was born. Vividly recall some of the highlights of his growing up. Remember the first day he rode a bike, the first day he drove a car, the night of his graduation. Picture yourself going up to the bride's parents, warmly shaking their hands and telling them how glad you are your son found someone he loves as much as he does their daughter. Picture yourself giving the bride a loving hug and congratulating her on her "good taste in men." Remember Dale Carnegie's advice that "we can make more friends in two months by becoming interested in other people, than we can in two years by trying to get people interested in us." Instead of being *self*-conscious and worrying about what *you* can say, picture yourself drawing others out and making sure they feel welcome. Imagine yourself thoroughly enjoying every moment of this once-in-a-lifetime special day. Choose to make this day something you'll happily reflect on for the rest of your life."

Martha sent a thank you card following her son's wedding and wrote, "The day was everything I could have hoped for." She went on to say, "You know, someone once told me that *worrying is praying for what you don't want*." I've realized that visualization is a way of praying for what you *do* want."

YOU TRY IT!

Remember at the beginning of this chapter (page 49) you wrote about a situation in which you would like to be more confident? It is time to design an action plan for how you're going to use visualization as a positive form of concentration to enhance your performance in that situation. Simply fill in the blanks that follow:

The situation in which I'd like to be more confident is

_____

_____

My fears, doubts, worries, or concerns about this situation are

_____

_____

Use the "professional comedian approach" and plan what you're going to do if any of these worries should happen. Prepare a response so you can handle even your worst fear with poise.

If _____ happens, I'm going to _____ .

_____

Now, look at your doubts and concerns. At this point, they are **irrelevant matters.** You are no longer going to waste time focusing on them. Instead, you are going to concentrate all your attention on what you *want to have happen* and/or how *you want to perform.*

When, where, and *how often* are you going to spend five minutes visualizing this situation?

_____

Specifically outline, using as many senses as possible and in sequential order, exactly how you're going to perform in this situation. I'm going to

_____

_____

Visualizing does not *guarantee success.* That would be an unrealistic promise. Visualizing does *guarantee improvement.* The time you spend positively concentrating on how you're going to perform *will* give you recent, frequent, successful practice which *will* make you perform better.

CHAPTER 6: "HOW CONCENTRATION WILL IMPROVE MY LISTENING, MEMORY, AND STUDYING SKILLS?"

> *"If you're not listening, you're not learning."*—Anonymous

You can change the above quote to, "If you're not concentrating, you're not listening." Listening, studying, and memorizing all involve concentration. They all require mastering the ability to focus and maintain attention on a chosen project. This chapter outlines concentration techniques you can use to improve the above skills, plus tips on how to teach others to concentrate. The following questionnaire will help you evaluate your present skill levels.

LISTENING

	SELDOM	SOMETIMES	OFTEN
1. My mind races ahead when someone else is speaking.	☐	☐	☐
2. I'm easily distracted and find it difficult to listen if someone talks for more than two to three minutes.	☐	☐	☐
3. I lean forward and adopt an attentive posture to help myself visually focus on the person who is speaking.	☐	☐	☐
4. I complete people's sentences for them, or help supply words or phrases they're having difficulty with.	☐	☐	☐
5. I think about what I would do or say if I were in the situation someone's talking about.	☐	☐	☐
6. I wait until someone's finished speaking before I judge whether or not their idea is a good one.	☐	☐	☐
7. My mind is so active I keep thinking of responses and I have to hold on to them so I don't forget them.	☐	☐	☐
8. I paraphrase back what I've heard to make sure I've understood what the speaker really meant.	☐	☐	☐
9. I try to put myself in the speaker's shoes to empathize.	☐	☐	☐

Listening Exercise Scoring Index

Score 5 points for Seldom, 3 for Sometimes, and 1 for Often answers to Questions 1, 2, 4, 5, 7.

Score 1 point for Seldom, 3 for Sometimes, and 5 for Often answers to Questions 3, 6, 8, 9.

Score Totals

35–45   Good for you! Not only do you have good listening and communication skills; you're probably popular everywhere you go!

25–34   Listening skills could be strengthened to improve relationships.

  0–24   Listen up! Make listening a priority. Commit to the L.I.S.T.E.N. acronym.

USING CONCENTRATION TO IMPROVE STUDY SKILLS

STUDYING	SELDOM	SOMETIMES	OFTEN
1. I clarify my purpose of studying before I begin.	☐	☐	☐
2. I stop every couple of pages to review what I've read and to ask "What of this will be asked on the test?"	☐	☐	☐
3. I use my highlighter sparingly and only underline really important points.	☐	☐	☐
4. If I have several subjects to study, I just start on the easiest first.	☐	☐	☐
5. I eliminate distractions (TV, radio) or remove myself from them so I can focus.	☐	☐	☐
6. I take breaks every 45 minutes to an hour to keep my comprehension and retention levels high.	☐	☐	☐
7. I clear my desk or study area so my eyes will not have things tempting or distracting them.	☐	☐	☐
8. I set up my environment so it *helps* me rather than *hurts* me (provide sufficient light, comfortable chair).	☐	☐	☐
9. I have a regular place where I study every time.	☐	☐	☐

Study Skills Scoring Index

Score 1 point for Seldom, 3 for Sometimes, and 5 for Often answers #1, 2, 3, 5, 6, 7, 8, 9.

Score 5 points for Seldom, 3 for Sometimes, and 1 for Often for answer #4.

Score Totals

35–45   Congratulations! You obviously know how to learn. Go for your Ph.D.!

25–34   By studying these study techniques, you'll get a lot better value for your time invested.

0–24   Hit the books! It's suggested that you read this section and do additional reading on the topic. You'll end up saving yourself a lot of time and getting dramatically improved results.

USING CONCENTRATION TO IMPROVE MEMORY SKILLS

MEMORY	SELDOM	SOMETIMES	OFTEN
1. I have a hard time remembering people's names.	☐	☐	☐
2. I forget where I put things (and have to search for my glasses, my purse or wallet).	☐	☐	☐
3. I use systems (acronyms, rhythm) to remember multiple items.	☐	☐	☐
4. I repeat things to imprint them for easier recall.	☐	☐	☐
5. If I give my mind an order to remember something, it will.	☐	☐	☐
6. I write down important reminders, so I'm sure not to forget them.	☐	☐	☐
7. I help myself remember things by linking them to something else so I can trigger recall through association.	☐	☐	☐
8. I review what I've read and heard to help imprint the information for better retention.	☐	☐	☐
9. If something is "on the tip of my tongue," I try to remember outstanding details of the situation, and the word or phrase I'm looking for "pops up."	☐	☐	☐

Memory Skills Scoring Index

Score 5 points for Seldom, 3 for Sometimes, and 1 for Often for answers #1 & 2.

Score 1 point for Seldom, 3 for Sometimes, and 5 for Often for answers #3, 4, 5, 6, 7, 8, 9.

Total Scores

35–45 You have a Masters in Memory!

25–34 You could make your life easier by practicing these memory techniques.

 0–24 Practice the C.A.R.S. system on a daily basis!

USING CONCENTRATION TO BECOME A BETTER LISTENER

Who is someone who *really* listens to you? _____

What specifically does that person *do* that makes them such a good listener? (Do they give you their total attention? Do they provide a good sounding board without giving unwanted advice?)

_____

_____

_____

How do *you* feel when this person listens to you?

_____

_____

_____

How do you feel about this person when they listen to you?

_____

_____

_____

Most people can usually think of only one or two individuals (of all the hundreds of people they know) who *really* listen to them. It's that rare. It's been said that "listening to someone is the single best way to make that person feel *significant*." By giving someone your attention you are saying, "You're the most important thing in my world right now. I could be thinking or doing something else. Instead, I'm choosing to focus on you." Becoming a better listener is one of the best things you can do to improve your relationship with anyone, plus it's a way to practice concentration on a daily basis.

LISTEN

The word LISTEN can be used as an acronym to remember six steps to becoming a more effective listener.

L = LOOK AND LEAN

Are you a parent? Have you ever been cooking or reading a newspaper, and your child has come up to you and said, "Mom or Dad?" You said, "Yes, dear, what do you want?" and continued to stir the soup or look at the paper. Your child probably tugged at your arm and said, "Mom, Mom, Dad, Dad." Maybe you replied, "Yes, dear, go ahead, I'm listening." But your child kept tugging and calling your name, *until you did what?* Probably until you stopped what you were doing, turned and looked at them. Children know your attention is "where your eyes are." The first rule of listening is to *attend with your eyes.*

You have probably heard the expression, "I was on the edge of my seat." When you want to hear what someone has to say, don't you almost automatically lean forward in your eagerness to listen? Whether you're sitting or standing, this is an excellent nonverbal way to let the other person know you're interested. Remember William James' observation that "it is easier to act ourselves into feeling, than it is to feel ourselves into acting?" Lean forward, raise your eyebrows in an expression of interest, put your eyes on the speaker's face, and you can **act** yourself into a state of attentiveness, even when you would rather be some place else.

I = IGNORE DISTRACTIONS

When someone says they're not a good listener, what they're really saying is they don't discipline themselves to concentrate on the person speaking. To really listen, you must consciously decide that what this person is saying is more important than anything else right now. There will always be things competing for your attention. If you determine that the person speaking is your top priority, then usher out any intruding thoughts by saying, "I'll think about that later (*after* this discussion is over, not *during*)." If you think of something you want to say or remember something you need to attend to, **jot it down** so it won't divide your attention.

LISTEN (Continued)

S = SUSPEND JUDGEMENT

Did you see the Academy Awards show the year Sir Lawrence Olivier received an award in honor of his lifelong achievements and contribution to the film industry? An amazing thing happened. A camera panned the audience and showed a number of people crying because they were so moved by his presentation. Afterwards, the emcee complimented Olivier on his acceptance speech and said it was the most eloquent presentation he'd ever heard. Olivier looked at him in astonishment and said, "You must be joking. That talk made no sense, I forgot what I was going to say!" The emcee didn't believe him so they rolled back the video tape and watched it. What Olivier said was true, he had been all over the map...referring to this director and then talking about something completely unrelated. If people had been listening, they would have been scratching their heads in bewilderment. But they weren't listening. They had *pre-judged* Olivier and they had become *caught up in his dramatic style.*

Is there anyone in your office who has a difficult "style"? When you see them coming down the hall, you think, "Oh no, it's ---!" and try to avoid them" Maybe there is someone who you've labeled as "the complainer." Do you have a friend who always seems to be asking favors? Is there a customer you dread dealing with because they talk in a whiny, irritating voice? It's easy to tune these people out because their personality or their style of speaking isn't very pleasant.

This may be the hardest part of being a good listener, but it's necessary if you really want to listen to these people. *Wait until they're finished talking before deciding* whether or not you agree with them, whether or not their idea has merit, whether or not you like them. It is said in a long-term relationship, you often start judging what the other person is saying based more on your history of them than on what it is they are actually saying. Remind yourself to **"give people a chance"** and concentrate on their content and meaning instead of tuning them out because you don't like the way they're saying it.

$\boxed{\text{T}}$ = TELL THEM WHAT YOU HEARD

Paraphrasing back to the speaker your understanding of what was said forces you to concentrate on what is being said. You can't afford to daydream if you want to play their message back correctly.

If you follow the rule that "before you can speak up for yourself, you must first summarize back to the other person what it is they just said to their satisfaction" you are *guaranteed* communication (defined in three words as the "exchange of meaning"). This may initially sound time-consuming and awkward, but people who commit to doing this can greatly reduce misunderstandings. Research has indicated that up to 60% of all mistakes at work are due to poor listening. As the saying goes, *"If you don't have time to do it right the first time, when are you going to have time to do it over again?"* Yes, paraphrasing does *take* time. In the long run though, it *saves* time!

Whenever communicating information that is important to get "right" (delegating tasks, giving directions, taking orders over the phone), help yourself and the other person concentrate by suggesting you both paraphrase to guarantee communication. So as not to imply they are not listening (which might insult them), diplomatically phrase this request by saying, "To make sure I explained this clearly, could you please tell me your understanding of how you're going to proceed on this project?"

Teachers often use a variation of this technique to help students concentrate in the classroom. They'll make sure everyone's paying attention by saying, "Now, repeat after me" or "All together now...."

LISTEN (Continued)

E = EXPERIENCE *THEIR* SIDE

It is easy to stop concentrating on what someone is saying when you've "heard that question a hundred times before" or because on some emotional level you don't like what they're saying. Your own agenda or frustration distracts you from really listening. You may think "Why doesn't he understand...?" or "Why didn't he...?" Have you ever stopped to realize what you're *really* saying whenever you start a statement about someone with the word "Why...?" What you're usually saying is, **"Why don't they do it the way I would?"** A wise professor once said, "Whenever you're frustrated or impatient with someone, it's usually because you're only seeing things from your point of view." Instead of becoming preoccupied or focusing on your own reactions, feel what they are feeling. Putting yourself in the other person's shoes is an excellent way to help yourself concentrate. It is also a characteristic that will endear you to other people because, as Eleanor Roosevelt once observed, "the essence of charm is having the ability to lose yourself in the other person."

When asked to explain a new policy for the umpteenth time, give yourself patience by thinking, "It may be the tenth time for me, but it's the first time for them!" If you're feeling exasperated with a customer because they're complaining about something that's not your fault, transcend your frustration by asking, "How would I feel if I were in their situation?" If you're in customer service, your chosen project is to "make every customer a return customer." Getting upset with a customer is an irrelevant matter because it distracts you from your goal of providing them with a favorable experience so they'll want to come back. Experiencing their side gives you empathy so you can concentrate on fixing the problem instead of getting upset with the problem.

 = NO INTERRUPTING

Ralph Nichols (a professor emeritus at the University of Minnesota who is often called the 'father of listening' because of more than thirty years research on this topic) was once asked if there was a secret to being a good listener. He thought about it for awhile and then said, ''There's no secret...it's hard work! It takes thinking and concentration. Plus, you have to bite your tongue once in awhile too.'' Our minds can think five to seven times faster than most people can speak which is why it's easy to ''race ahead'' and finish people's statements for them. From now on, if you want to check if you're really concentrating on what someone is saying, just ask yourself, *''Am I really listening, or am I just waiting for my turn to talk?''*

Some people rush from the moment they wake up until the moment they go to bed. As a result, they're sometimes impatient with the important people in their lives. When someone wants to talk to them, their response is, ''I don't have time right now, can we talk about this later?'' or ''Hurry up, we're going to be late.'' Their loved ones can end up feeling they don't matter.

Are you leading a busy life? Time isn't running—you are!! You can partially make up for a full schedule by taking the time at least once a day to really listen to the people you care about. Sit down with them for a minimum of five minutes (with children it's especially important to get down on their level); look them in the eye; and then just—listen. No interrupting, no looking at your watch, no frowns or exasperated looks, no suggestions of what you think they ought to do. Give them your full attention. It's a way to say **''you're important''** and it can compensate for a lot of the times you seem preoccupied and perpetually ''on the go.'' Plus it's a great way to keep your concentration skills ''in shape.''

EXERCISE: LISTENING

Who is someone in your life who deserves to receive some good listening from you?

_____

_____

_____

_____

_____

_____

_____

What is a bad habit or practice you've fallen into when listening to this person?

_____

_____

_____

_____

_____

_____

_____

What is one specific thing you're going to do to be a better listener the next time you sit down with this person for a discussion?

_____

_____

_____

_____

_____

_____

IMPROVING YOUR MEMORY THROUGH CONCENTRATION

The purpose of this section is to focus specifically on how you can use the C.C.A.R.S. system to improve your retention and recall of information. The C.C.A.R.S. acronym can be used to "remember how to remember" important information. Since many people feel they are "terrible" at remembering names, this system will focus specifically on how to use C.C.A.R.S. to remember names.

 = COMMIT

Are you good at remembering names? A majority of people don't think they are. It's not that they *can't*, it's just that they haven't *made up their minds* that this is something important they want to do. Remembering doesn't just happen. You have to give your mind what's called a "determining tendency." In other words, you need to make a conscious commitment to remember names. How do you feel when someone remembers your name? Probably you are flattered. It indicates you were important enough for them to make the effort to remember. How do you feel about people who can remember names? If you think of them in a positive way decide right now that this is something you're going to "get good at."

 = CONCENTRATE

When you're being introduced to someone, do you automatically screen out that person's name? Not concentrating is called "failure forecasting." Think of all the people whose names you've forgotten simply because you told your mind it wasn't important. From now on, "prognosticate positively." Tell your mind what you want it to do. Make each new person you meet to be a "chosen project." Decide that any distracting thoughts is *irrelevant*. From now on, whenever you meet people, say to yourself, "I'm going to remember these people's names." It is a good way to keep your concentration skills "in condition," and it is a social grace that will serve you and others well.

IMPROVING YOUR MEMORY THROUGH CONCENTRATION (Continued)

 = ATTENTION

Your attention is where your eyes are. It's vital to focus your eyes fully on the person's face when they say their name, so the two will be linked in your mind. No looking over their shoulder at who just came in the room. No nodding to a friend who's trying to get your attention. For the five or ten seconds it takes to exchange names, look them "in the eye" to preclude preoccupation. Shaking hands helps cement and personalize introductions because it causes you to lean forward which *physically* singles out that individual for your attention. This is especially important in a noisy, crowded room. The touch of a handshake literally and figuratively connects the two of you when otherwise you might be visually distracted or not hear what they're saying.

 = REPETITION

Repeat the person's name out loud as soon as you hear it. Then repeat it to yourself at least three times in *spaced* intervals. Repetition is important for several reasons. First, you want to make sure you've heard the name correctly (e.g., Rob not Bob, Betty as opposed to Betsy). Secondly, the more senses you use to imprint information, the more likely you are to recall it. If you're *hearing* the name and *saying* the name while *looking* at their face, you will be giving your mind several hooks on which to hang a memory. Obviously, if you're in a situation where it's appropriate to write down the names of the people you've met (and a word or two about your conversation), that will enhance recall even more. Physiologists believe your ability to recall information depends on whether or not is has been "reviewed" at different times with "wait" periods in between. This signals the mind that the date is a "keeper" (important enough to store) and it's entered into long-term memory. The next time you see that person, their name should "pop" into your mind.

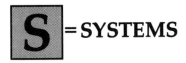 **= SYSTEMS**

A variety of systems (e.g., associations, establishing patterns, visualizing, and repeating things in rhyme or with a rhythmic beat) can help further enhance your recall of important items.

Associations are when you link something *new* to something *familiar*. Maggie Bedrosian, a respected professional speaker, helps people remember her last name by saying, "Think of a bed of roses."

Establishing patterns means always doing something the same way so you don't have to recall random actions. You can remember where you put your keys by vowing right now to always keep them in the same spot (e.g., in the outside zippered pocket of your purse, or in the bowl by the front door). No exceptions!

Visualizing can be used to plant a mental picture to trigger a specific memory. If you want to remember where you left your car at the airport, (and you don't have time to write it down), just vividly imagine in your mind getting off the plane, retracing your steps back into the parking lot, looking for the pole with the letter E in the right hand corner of the lot, and walking over to your car parked under the sign. If you're about to go to sleep and you hear a weather report predicting rain for the next day, repeatedly picture a big umbrella by the front door and see yourself grabbing it as you leave for work. The next morning as you leave for work, voila!

Rythym and rhymes are how children learn the alphabet and sing-along songs. If you're standing in a phone booth and you get someone's number from the information operator and you want to remember it long enough to get your quarter in the slot, just put the seven digits into a "rap"...fourfivefive...eleven thirty eight. Fourfivefive...eleven thirty eight. You'll be amazed at how easily you can remember numbers with this method.

Acronyms can help you remember lists of multiple, seemingly unrelated items. Just as you can use the C.C.A.R.S. system to "remember how to remember," you can use acronyms to remember anything.

IMPROVING YOUR MEMORY THROUGH CONCENTRATION (Continued)

Shirley, a busy executive, remarked, "Sometimes I go to two or three meetings a day. There are weeks when I meet hundreds of people! I've realized I will never be able to remember *every*one's name. With this C.C.A.R.S. system though... I'll remember *more* of them!" Isn't that the point? You'll never have a perfect memory. Using these concentration techniques however can help you remember *more* of what's important to you.

One final note about memory. William, an older individual confessed he was worried because he was becoming so forgetful. He said he would run into people he had known for years and not be able to remember their names. He recently spent thirty minutes looking for his glasses before he found them on the top of his head! He used to be a successful stockbroker, and it really bothered him that he was "losing" his "mental powers." When asked what activities in his life required concentration, he said he played golf, enjoyed working around his house, and playing with his grandchildren.

William needed to realize the saying **"use it or lose it!"** is as true of memory as it is physical conditioning. Concentration and memory are *skills*. Just as school study skills get rusty over summer vacations, Wiliam's concentration and memory skills will backslide unless they are practiced on a regular basis. He decided to re-introduce activities like crossword puzzles, card games, chess, and challenging reading. He smiled and said, "I never thought of it that way, but I've let my mental muscles get *flabby!* I'm going to start exercising my mind at least once a day so it stays **fit!**"

What is an occasion coming up where you will be meeting people? Give yourself a "determining tendency" to remember the names of the people you meet. Writing this down will help you act on your good intentions. When I go to _____ I'm going to remember people's names by _____

_____

One "system" I'm going to use to start remembering things is (e.g., I'm going to use a pattern to remember where I put my credit cards. Starting today, I will always put them in the snapped enclosure of my wallet) _____

_____

IMPROVING STUDY SKILLS THROUGH CONCENTRATION

Are you thinking of taking a class to improve your skills and knowledge? It's ironic that only recently have people started understanding they have to "learn how to learn." Studying effectively is a skill in itself. By learning how to do it properly, you can maximize the time you spend "hitting the books." Concentration tips can help improve your performance on tests and can increase your comprehension and retention of any reading or research you might do in the line of your work.

Always *plan* your study time and establish a clear *purpose*. Use the following checklist every time you sit down to study.

A. What subjects do you need to spend time on? _____

_____

B. What is your *purpose*? For each one? It's inefficient to just "study"—what are you studying "*for*"?

_____

_____

C. How much time do you estimate it will take for each subject?

_____

D. Which is your most difficult subject **or** the subject that is most important tonight (Do you have a test on that subject the next day, a paper to be turned in?)

_____

_____

E. What is your easiest subject or the subject that will require the least effort tonight?

_____

F. When will your study environment be *most* conducive to concentrating (fewest distractions, noise, or interruptions) and when will it be *least* conducive to concentrating?

_____

G. When will your energy level be *best* during the time you've scheduled for study, and when will your mental feet be dragging?

_____

IMPROVING STUDY SKILLS THROUGH CONCENTRATION (Continued)

Knowing the importance of concentration to performance, set up your study time so you use your mental energy *judiciously*. To the degree possible, schedule your *hardest* (or most important topic) when your energy level will be highest and when your environment will be *most* conducive to study. Schedule your *easiest* (or favorite) topic for when the study environment and your energy level are *least* optimal. Always try to study at the same desk or table. Just as walking into a kitchen can prompt thoughts of food, sitting at your desk can trigger thoughts of study.

A student said this system helped him make a radical improvement in his grades. Before he started using this **STUDEE** system (**S**tudy **T**opics **U**sing **D**ifficulty, **E**nvironment, and **E**nergy), he had fallen into a habit of studying what he *liked* first. He had at least two hours of homework every night. By the time he got to his least favorite topic, he'd be so mentally tired that the problems took twice as long to solve as they should have. Sometimes he'd just quit in frustration. He now has committed himself to use this system so he's at his sharpest with his toughest subjects. He works on the subject he likes best last, so his natural interest will make up for any mental fatigue. He's motivated to keep using the system because he ends up spending *less* time studying, gets better results, and has more time for recreation.

BEFORE USING THE STUDEE SYSTEM

TEACHING OTHERS TO CONCENTRATE

Are you a parent, teacher, manager, or coach? Would you like to help other people acquire the ability to "stay on task?" Use the A.H.A. system outlined below to help the people you care about develop the ability to focus and maintain their attention, despite boredom and frustration.

 = AWARENESS

You wouldn't expect anyone to be able to play a piano unless they had been given opportunities to play and take lessons. Likewise, if you want someone to have the ability to concentrate, he or she must be introduced to the concept and be given "training" in it. Start using the word around your home, in the classroom, at work, or on the playing field. Start talking about how important concentration is to performing well, winning, and attaining desired goals. Look for situations where someone succeeded because they didn't mentally "give up." Discuss these with others so they can see how it would be to their benefit to learn this valuable skill. Ben Franklin's observation that "a good example is the best sermon" still holds true. The best way to positively influence others and to convince them of the value of concentration is to *model* it yourself.

 = HONOR

Set up an environment in which concentration is honored. Many well-meaning parents unintentionally interfere with their child's natural ability to focus. A father realized he sometimes unthinkingly disrupted his little boys' concentration. His youngest son would be drawing, and in the father's eagerness to help, he would bring over some other crayons and say, "Here are some different colors." Or he would call, "Time for supper!" and his other son would ask, "Can I have a few more minutes, Dad? I'm almost finished with my homework." He would insist, "No, dinner is right now!" Concentration can be a fragile state of mind that is difficult to acquire. Practice **concentration courtesy**. Before interrupting someone who is obviously deeply involved in something, ask yourself, "Is what I'm going to say all that important or urgent?" If not, maybe it can wait. The delay might not matter much to you, but it can make a big difference to someone who has momentum in what they're doing. For people at work and in the classroom, make it a standing rule that people use their "mental manners."

THE A.H.A. SYSTEM (Continued)

 **= ACCOUNTABLE**

> *"Nothing in the world can take the place of persistence. Talent will not; nothing is more common than unsuccessful men with talent. Genius will not; unrewarded genius is almost a proverb. Education will not; the world is full of educated derelicts. Persistence and determination alone are omnipotent."*—Calvin Coolidge

Concentration is mental persistence. How can you help other people develop this valuable charactistic? *By holding them accountable for finishing projects—even when they don't want to.* What if a child is working on a puzzle or a difficult math problem, gets discouraged, says "I quit," and gets up to leave? Say, "I understand you're frustrated. Let's sit back down and work on this some more. If you keep working, you'll be able to finish it, and won't that feel good?" On the job, if employees come to you with difficult situations, don't rescue them! Rushing to their aid actually "rewards" their giving up and they will grow to depend on you for help whenever they encounter anything complicated. Instead of owning their problem and solving it for them (e.g., "I feel this is the best way to handle it" or "I suggest...", offer guidance by asking questions with the word "you" (e.g., "Do you think this will work?" or "Could you...?") Accomplishment is measured by the number of *completed* assignments—not the number of assignments *started*. Holding people responsible for their work commitments will help them develop self-sufficient concentration—the discipline to persevere and *complete* challenging assignments.

Ralph Waldo Emerson once said, "We all are looking for someone who will make us do what we can." You may not be particularly popular when you hold someone accountable for finishing projects. In the long run though, they will be indebted to you for helping them develop mental toughness and character. Mental toughness is the ability to concentrate past the point of mental and/or physical exhaustion. Character is having the commitment to carry out resolutions—*when the mood they were made in is gone.* What a wonderful gift to give someone!

PART IV

No More Excuses

CHAPTER 7: "WHAT IF I'M TOO TIRED TO CONCENTRATE?"

> "Concentration is a form of *directed mental energy.*"

What if you're tired, under stress, or ill? You can *give* yourself energy, and learn how to use your available energy economically with the following **ENERGY IDEAS**.

ENERGY IDEA #1: *Complete this simple exercise to identify "problems" that could be stealing your energy.*

Have you ever played word association games? Someone asks you a question and you say the first thing that pops into your mind. It's important not to second-guess your answer because that might stifle your response. Your first thought is usually the most honest one and that is what you want. The exercise on the following page is a variation of a word association game. Your responses can help identify problems that might be "stealing" your energy and undermining your ability to concentrate.

EXERCISE: CONCENTRATION

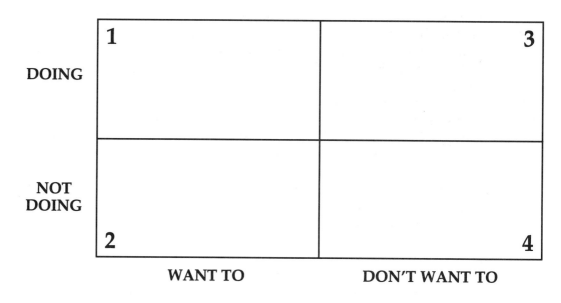

	WANT TO	DON'T WANT TO
DOING	**1**	**3**
NOT DOING	**2**	**4**

INSTRUCTIONS

Write in Square 1 your first response to this question: *What are you doing in your life that you want to?* (e.g., you're taking ballroom dancing lessons, living in a small, friendly town, taking professional development classes). In other words, what are you doing that's satisfying to you?

Write in Square 2 your first response to this question: *What are you **not** doing in your life that you want to?* (e.g., not exercising, not spending enough time with your family, not traveling). In other words, what do you wish you were doing and you're not?

Write in Square 3 your first response to this question: *What are you doing in your life that you **don't** want to?* (e.g. fighting with your spouse, working eighty hours a week, commuting fifty miles every day). In other words, what is happening in your life that you wish wasn't?

Write in Square 4 your first response to this question: *What are you **not** doing in your life that you **don't** want to?* Yes, this is a double negative. It's an important question though because it identifies those things you *really* don't want to do, and are currently keeping out of your life. (e.g., you don't want to work for someone else, don't want to live in a crime-ridden neighborhood, don't want to have to work two jobs).

Take an extra five minutes and go back to fill in additional responses. Your initial responses are most important, but others can provide additional insights.

NEXT STEPS

When you're finished, circle the answers you wrote in Squares 2 and 3. These are your **problems.** These situations are what's wrong with your life. They could be draining your spirit and occupying your mind. A statesman once said, "The mark of a successful organization isn't whether or not it has problems, it's whether it has the *same* problems it had last year." Just replace the word "organization" with "individual" and that statement may have insight for you. The question isn't whether or not you have problems in your life; the question is how *long* have you had those problems and how much are they *troubling* you? Could they be monopolizing your energy and undermining your ability to concentrate?

One woman reported this exercise helped her confront an issue that had undermined her concentration to the point she thought she was losing her mind. Someone would be talking to her and she wouldn't even hear them. She had several "near-misses" while driving because she wasn't paying attention to where she was going. She would stare at paperwork but couldn't motivate herself to start working on it. When she answered the question in Square 2, she realized that what she was *not doing* that she *wanted to* was be with her mom who was dying of cancer. They had been very close all their lives, and not having the time or the money to fly back to take care of her filled her with despair. Her problem wasn't that she *couldn't* concentrate. Her problem was she was not taking action to resolve a situation that was debilitating her emotionally. Once she realized this she approached her boss and explained the situation. He arranged for the company to advance three months salary and give her a month off without pay so she could spend time with her mother. By taking action on the real underlying source of her problem, she was able to start functioning normally again.

WHAT IF I'M TOO TIRED TO CONCENTRATE? (Continued)

ENERGY IDEA #2: *Assign bothersome, attention-destroying thoughts a worry time!*

If you try and banish a problem (''I will *not* think about that now'') or helplessly say ''I just can't get my mind off...''; it will continue to occupy your thoughts. The mind cannot concentrate on the *reverse* of an idea (e.g., ''I will not make that mistake twice,'' ''I won't let that happen again,'' or ''I'm never going to procrastinate again.'') By promising yourself instead, ''I want to resolve this *and* will think about it tonight'' or ''I need to decide what to do *and* I'll sit down at 3:00 and discuss it in detail'' your mind will become ''free from worry'' for the moment and can return to your original project. It is true we can't always control what comes into our mind. We can control how long it stays there however. Make your mind a deal it can't refuse. The mind will ''leave it be for now'' if it knows it's going to have a chance to consider it later.

ENERGY IDEA #3: *Promote mental fitness by being physically fit.*

Are you consistently tired? An ironic paradox is the *less* active you are, the *less* energy you have. Inactivity leads to depression, which leads to more inactivity, which leads to depression, and so forth. Aerobic exercise three times a week for twenty minutes a session will boost energy and concentration. If you're in the middle of an afternoon going ''stale,'' treat yourself to a brisk five minute walk. If you're at home, take a refreshing shower. If you're facing an evening of paperwork and are already exhausted; the best thing you can do is take some exercise before going home. You may initially feel ''too tired'' to exercise but it will pay off by giving you *more* energy than when you started!

ENERGY IDEA #4: *Talk yourself into eagerness* instead of *exhaustion.*

Abraham Lincoln said, ''Most people are about as happy as they make up their minds to be.'' The same is true about being tired. *Most people are about as tired as they make up their minds to be.* Actors and actresses know they can ''talk'' themselves into feeling and projecting an emotion (fear, anger, joy) by simply repeating the corresponding words to themselves. From now on, instead of talking yourself into exhaustion (e.g., ''I'm beat,'' ''I'm really dragging,'') talk yourself into *enthusiasm* (I'm looking forward to this,'' ''I have energy to spare,'' ''I can't wait to get started''). This positive self talk will give you an energy boost that you can direct towards your chosen project.

ENERGY IDEA #5: *Take breaks to rest and refresh your mind.*

When Mark Twain observed, ''No sinner was ever saved after the first twenty minutes of a sermon,'' he must have known that the attention span of most people is twenty minutes. After reading, writing, watching or listening for twenty minutes, concentration starts to wander. After that point, comprehension and retention start to deteriorate and don't recover until the mind gets a rest, or until the mind encounters something personally relevant. Avoid working for extended periods of time because the Law of Diminishing Returns means you will not get good value from your time investment. Instead of working ''straight through,'' take a few minutes every so often to get up and walk around.'

ENERGY IDEA #6: *Conserve energy by using routines.*

How can professional golfers concentrate for an entire five hour round? They don't. If you watch Lee Trevino, he relaxes until it is his turn. Then he uses a *pre-shot routine* to get down to business and concentrate. His *ritual* consists of addressing the ball in the same way, visualizing a smooth stroke, and then doing it. Once he makes his shot, he ''turns off his concentration'' and relaxes until it is time for the next shot. How could tennis great Jimmy Connors argue with an umpire and then be the picture of concentration a few seconds later? His routine was to bounce the ball four times before he served, his way of ordering his mind to ''get serious.'' If you are in an on-going situation, don't expect to be able to concentrate the entire time. Develop a procedure that you repeat the same way every time so you can concentrate on command. By being able to turn your mental ''faucet'' on and off, your energy reservoir won't run dry.

ENERGY IDEA #7: *Take* action *to resolve the* real *source of your lack of energy.*

A teacher walked into her classroom and found a big puddle on the floor. She called the janitor and he mopped it up. The next day there was another puddle in the same place. She called the janitor and he mopped it up again. When she walked in the third morning and found another puddle, she called the maintenance superintendent and asked him to take care of the puddle. When he showed up he didn't have a mop. The teacher asked, ''How are you going to mop up the puddle?'' He just said, ''I'm not. *I'm going to fix the leak!*''

When you can't concentrate, do you mop up the puddle, or do you fix the leak? If you have a bad case of ''brain cramp,'' what do you do? Do you try harder, tighten your jaw, and tell yourself to concentrate, or do you give up? All of these responses are ways of mopping up the puddle. They don't do anything to solve your energy problem. Get more sleep, more exercise, more healthy foods, more positive self talk...and that will supply the energy you need.

ENERGY EXERCISE

Is there a "leak" in your life? Is there an answer you gave in square 2 or 3 that may be compromising your ability to concentrate? A "problem" that's been depleting my energy is

_____

_____

How have you been mopping up the floor? (e.g., Maybe you've been going in early so you could get work done without being interrupted, you've been drinking cup after cup of coffee to keep yourself awake at your job because you haven't been getting enough sleep.) Because I've not been able to concentrate, I've

_____

_____

_____

How are you going to fix the leak? (e.g., You're going to start diplomatically deflecting lower-priority conversations (instead of suffering in silence); you're going to document that your workload is too heavy and negotiate with your boss for a reduction in duties instead of working eighty hours a week; you're going to call up your old-time running buddy and ask him to start jogging with you in the mornings again instead of constantly feeling fatigued.) I'm going to

_____

_____

_____

CHAPTER 8: "WHAT IF I'VE NEVER BEEN ABLE TO CONCENTRATE?"

Of all the factors that determine whether or not you're able to concentrate, *attitude* is the most important. You can have privacy and an absence of distractions, you can have a clear goal, you can even have an interest in the task; but if you think you can't concentrate, you'll be right! Thomas Jefferson said, "Nothing can stop the man with the right mental attitude from achieving his goal; nothing on earth can help the man with the wrong mental attitude. Set yourself up for success by using the following **attitude adjusters**.

ATTITUDE ADJUSTER #1   *Putting labels in the past*

Do you have any labels for yourself relating to concentration? Do you see yourself as absent-minded? Do you claim you can't remember names? Do you feel you "fall apart" under stress? Do you say things like "No one could concentrate in that crazy office?" Many limiting labels are gross distortions of one failed or traumatic experience. (e.g., on any given day an individual remembers hundreds of things. Yet, if he forgets the name of one person, or misplaces one item, he gets upset and calls himself forgetful.)

Have you heard of an old world method used to train elephants? Initially, an elephant's back leg would be tied to a stake buried deep in the ground. After days of trying to break free, the elephant would realize it was not possible and would give up. At that point, the trainer can tie the elephant to a flimsy pin in the ground with just a thin rope. If the elephant wanted to, it could easily snap the rope and be free, but it doesn't even try to because the elephant *"knows"* it can't.

Do you ever limit your ability to concentrate with a similar delusion? Maybe you say "I'll never be able to figure out those computers" because you took a LOTUS 1-2-3 class several years ago and ended up withdrawing because it was just too complicated. Maybe you say "I choke under pressure" because a long time ago in a tournament you became so aware of people watching that you ended up blowing a big lead and losing.

WHAT IF I'VE NEVER BEEN ABLE TO CONCENTRATE? (Continued)

Labels

From now on, preface any labels you might have about yourself with:

"In the past _____"

"Up until now _____"

"I used to _____"

"Before I _____"

Follow them up with:

"and now I _____"

"from now on I _____"

"this time I'm going to _____"

"next time I _____"

For example, "I used to be a terrible listener, but now I give full attention to the person speaking and try to put myself in their shoes. Or, in the past, I got frazzled because I tried to do too many things at once. Now I keep a short list of my seven most important priorities, and focus on getting the most important thing done first." Fill in the blanks above with any *former* limiting labels you had and write down the *new* self talk you're going to use to set-up (instead of sabotage) concentration.

ATTITUDE ADJUSTER #2   *Choose to focus on the future instead of the past*

What if you're disappointed with your performance? What if you're really concentrating, and something goes wrong? You have two options. The option you choose will determine whether the mistake causes a *temporary* or *permanent* lapse in your concentration.

The options are: do you choose to focus on the *past*

or

do you choose to focus on the *future?*

If you choose to focus on the past ("How could I have done that? I can't believe I said that! What was I thinking of! I should have prepared better!") your performance will deteriorate because you will no longer be giving 100% attention to your chosen project.

Choose instead to focus on the future. What do you *want* to have happen from here on out? What are you *going* to do? (e.g., ''From now on I'm going to think twice before speaking up'' or ''I'm going to spend a half hour rehearsing my presentation next time.'')

On any given day in sports, one can find example after example of athletes who were playing well and then something ''bad'' happened (e.g., they received a questionable call, they shot a double bogie, they misjudged the finish line, they dropped an easy catch). If they *let* it get to them, they lost their concentration and their performance suffered. If they shrugged it off, extracted the value from it, and turned their full attention to what they were going to do next (e.g., ''I'm going to keep my head down this time'' or ''From now on, I'm going to keep my eye on the ball''), they maintained their concentation and their mistakes actually shaped improved performance.

Remember, no one ever learned by trial and ''right.'' You are going to make mistakes. When you do, what's it going to be? Are you going to focus on the *past*, or concentrate on the *future?*

ATTITUDE ADJUSTER #3 *Mental glass jaw::* Distractions don't cause stress— our reactions to distractions cause stress.

Eleanor Roosevelt said ''no one can make you feel inferior without your consent.'' This can be modified to say *''No one can break your concentration without your consent.''* If you are really ''cooking'' on a project and someone interrupts, it's your choice whether or not to get perturbed. Even if you've had a mental ''glass jaw'' until now (one hit and your attention is gone); you can learn to control your concentration temper. If the telephone rings, instead of getting exasperated (''darn that phone, now I'll never get my momentum back''), mark your place, calmly handle the call, and simply pick up the flow of your original assignment. The more emotion you give to a disruption (an irrelevant matter) the more it will disrupt your concentration. A fundamental concept of stress management is that ''events don't cause stress; our interpretation of events causes stress.'' Distractions in and of themselves don't have the power to destroy your concentration—unless you give them that power.

WHAT IF I'VE NEVER BEEN ABLE TO CONCENTRATE? (Continued)

> **ATTITUDE ADJUSTER #4** *You can't always choose or control your circumstances. You can control how you respond to them.*

The front desk manager for a large hotel told of the time she was confronted by an angry guest who unleashed a torrent of verbal abuse at her. Judy's mind took the guest "home" with her that night (i.e., he might as well have really been there) because she got upset all over again reliving the experience. That night she couldn't even concentrate on reading the newspaper because she was still thinking about what the guest had said. She told her husband, "The nerve of that man. He makes me so mad!" Her husband calmly asked, "Judy, what time is it?" She looked at him, rather taken aback, and said, "It's seven o'clock." He said, "What time did this happen?" Judy said, "At nine o'clock this morning." Her husband asked, "Judy, is that man the person who's making you angry? He isn't even here. *You're* the one who is allowing yourself to be so upset."

Judy could have benefitted from Victor Frankl's book, *Man's Search For Meaning*, an account of his experiences in a concentration camp and the philosophy he and other survivors developed as a result of those experiences. In it, he concluded, "Our greatest freedom is the freedom to *choose our attitude.*" This is true, isn't it? **We can't always choose or control our circumstances, but we choose how to respond to them.**

From the beginning of time, people have used concentration to transcend their circumstances. Stories abound of people achieving "super-human" feats (lifting cars off injured children, driving for 36 hours to get to the bedside of an ailing friend) because they were totally focused. Mothers giving birth can "block out pain" (to a degree!) by giving their minds a *different* focal point (breathing) and mentally locking on to it. Prisoners during wartime helped themselves endure years of captivity in horrible conditions by "going home in their minds." By concentrating on family, friends and good times, they could mentally escape from their surroundings.

> **ATTITUDE ADJUSTER #5** *Concentrate on what you have instead of on what you don't have. Be grateful instead of grumpy.*

What circumstances in your life don't you choose or control? Maybe you don't choose to work in a cramped, busy office with desks jammed together, but that's what your work area is like. Maybe you don't control the behavior of some of the difficult customers you have to deal with. Just as Judy "chose" to ruin her evening by concentrating on an argument that had taken place ten hours earlier, some people choose to dwell on distractions and end up ruining their work efforts. Some people choose to focus on their mistakes and end up compromising their performance. Some people choose to focus on their doubts and fears and end up undermining their confidence. Some people choose to focus on the obstacles in their path and end up never getting what they want.

People tend to waste what they don't value. Do you value time? Do you value your health? One of the best uses of concentration is to choose positive (rather than negative) mind sets. From now on, why don't you choose to focus on the benefits of achieving your chosen projects, instead of the difficulties? Focus on the future, instead of what's gone wrong in the past. Clarify what's most important to you and concentrate your attention and energies on your true priorities, instead of frittering away precious time on trivialities. Appreciate what you have, instead of dwelling on what you don't have. See life as an accumulation of treasures, rather than a series of trials and tribulations.

An older woman came up after a presentation and said, "I had a stroke last year and I realize I've been using it as an excuse for letting my mind go to mush. I blame my stroke whenever I forget something. I say it's why I'm not interested in doing things anymore. It was not my choice to have a stroke. But I did. I realize it *is* my choice how to respond to it. Instead of feeling sorry for myself, I've decided to **choose** to appreciate the fact that I'm still around! I *can* concentrate...if I *put my mind to it!*" She smiled when she realized what she had just said. Smart woman!!

FAILURE IS THE PATH OF LEAST PERSISTENCE

ATTITUDE ADJUSTER #6   *Failure is the path of least persistence.*

Aviation pioneer Chuck Yeager said ''At the 'moment of truth' there will either be *reasons* or *results*.'' There will always be reasons why it will be difficult for you to concentrate. There will be distractions, the sun will be in your eyes, it'll be too noisy, you won't be interested in your task, you'll be tired. If you choose to use these as excuses, you'll never get your desired results. *Failure is the path of least persistence. Make up your mind* (a determining tendency that leads to concentration) to achieve your chosen projects—no matter what! Your mental determination will produce rewards that will enrich the rest of your life.

A person/situation that used to make me mad and undermine my ability to focus was

_____

From now on, I'm going to *choose* to not give that person/situation the power to unsettle me. Next time I'm around that person or in that situation, I'm going to

_____

_____

An excuse I've been using for not being able to concentrate is

_____

From now on, I'm going to get results (instead of give reasons) by

_____

Something I really want to accomplish is (e.g., get my pilot's license, travel to Europe, start my own business).

_____

Are you *interested* or *committed*? If you're committed, write ''I'm going to

_____

_____—no matter what!''

(e.g., ''I'm going to start my own business—no matter what!'') Concentrate all your mental powers on achieving your goal. If you persist, you will succeed!

SUMMARY

> *"Happiness isn't a goal; it's a by-product"*—Eleanor Roosevelt

Concentration isn't a goal; it's a by-product. It's a by-product of following up and using the five most important ideas of this book. If you're not able to concentrate in a situation, go ahead and get M.M.M.A.D.! (This acronym of the five steps to concentration is the *only* time it will *help* you get mad!)

M = *Manage your environment.* Diplomatically impose on time, people, and events your decision as to what's important and what must come first. Courteously control, minimize, and deflect distractions and interruptions. Organize your work area so it's conducive to concentration.

M = *Mentally prepare.* Give your mind an order and establish one clear purpose (chosen project). Visualize to give yourself a mental road map and to improve confidence and performance. Trigger concentraton with a routine or ritual.

M = *Motivate yourself.* Put yourself into a "want to concentrate" frame of mind through positive self talk, by focusing on the benefits, establihsing deadlines to give yourself a sense of urgency, dividing up overwhelming projects, and by *starting* (even when you don't feel like it).

A = *Approach positively.* You can concentrate—if you think you can. Put limiting labels in the past with "I used to...." Choose to focus on results rather than reasons, on the future instead of the past.

D = *Develop the skill.* Practice the five minute affirmation exercise so you acquire the ability to focus and maintain attention—no matter what! Keep your concentration skills "current" by really listening and by exercising your mind with activities that require mental discipline.

ACTION PLAN

"The object of education isn't knowledge, it's *action!*"

Wanting to concentrate won't produce results. *Learning how* to concentrate won't produce results. Only *using these concentration techniques* will produce results.

Are you thinking "There's so much information here, I don't know where to start?" Set yourself up for success (and practice what's been preached in this book) by choosing *a specific project* on which you intend to follow up. Clarity leads to action. Select just *one* idea that's been particularly timely or relevant for you. What is the idea? Why is it meaningful to you?

_____

_____

_____

_____

_____

How *exactly* are you going to use this idea? Be specific and explain all the "w's" (When are you going to do this? Where will you use this? Who are you going to use this with? What are you going to say or not say?)

_____

_____

_____

_____

_____

A final word. Recipes don't make cookies! This recipe for concentration works, if you do! Remember, you *can* concentrate—if you put your mind to it!

CONCENTRATION CLINIC GRADUATE!

NOTES

NOTES

NOTES

NOTES

NOW AVAILABLE FROM
CRISP PUBLICATIONS

Books • Videos • CD Roms • Computer-Based Training Products

If you enjoyed this book, we have great news for you. There are over 200 books available in the *50-Minute*™ Series. To request a free full-line catalog, contact your local distributor or Crisp Publications, Inc., 1200 Hamilton Court, Menlo Park, CA 94025. Our toll-free number is 800-422-7477.

Subject Areas Include:

Management

Human Resources

Communication Skills

Personal Development

Marketing/Sales

Organizational Development

Customer Service/Quality

Computer Skills

Small Business and Entrepreneurship

Adult Literacy and Learning

Life Planning and Retirement

CRISP WORLDWIDE DISTRIBUTION

English language books are distributed worldwide. Major international distributors include:

ASIA/PACIFIC

Australia/New Zealand: In Learning, PO Box 1051 Springwood QLD, Brisbane, Australia 4127
Telephone: 7-3841-1061, Facsimile: 7-3841-1580   ATTN: Messrs. Gordon

Singapore: Graham Brash (Pvt) Ltd. 32, Gul Drive, Singapore 2262
Telphone: 65-861-1336, Facsimile: 65-861-4815   ATTN: Mr. Campbell

CANADA

Reid Publishing, Ltd., Box 69559-109 Thomas Street, Oakville, Ontario Canada L6J 7R4.
Telephone: (905) 842-4428, Facsimile: (905) 842-9327   ATTN: Mr. Reid

Trade Book Stores: Raincoast Books, 8680 Cambie Street, Vancouver, British Columbia, Canada V6P 6M9.
Telephone: (604) 323–7100, Facsimile: 604-323-2600   ATTN: Ms. Laidley

EUROPEAN UNION

England: Flex Training, Ltd. 9-15 Hitchin Street, Baldock, Hertfordshire, SG7 6A, England
Telephone: 1-462-896000, Facsimile: 1-462-892417   ATTN: Mr. Willetts

INDIA

Multi-Media HRD, Pvt., Ltd., National House, Tulloch Road, Appolo Bunder, Bombay, India 400-039
Telephone: 91-22-204-2281, Facsimile: 91-22-283-6478   ATTN: Messrs. Aggarwal

MIDDLE EAST

United Arab Emirates: Al-Mutanabbi Bookshop, PO Box 71946, Abu Dhabi
Telephone: 971-2-321-519, Facsimile: 971-2-317-706   ATTN: Mr. Salabbai

SOUTH AMERICA

Mexico: Grupo Editorial Iberoamerica, Serapio Rendon #125, Col. San Rafael, 06470 Mexico, D.F.
Telephone: 525-705-0585, Facsimile: 525-535-2009   ATTN: Señor Grepe

SOUTH AFRICA

Alternative Books, Unit A3 Sanlam Micro Industrial Park, Hammer Avenue STRYDOM Park, Randburg, 2194 South Africa
Telephone: 2711 792 7730, Facsimile: 2711 792 7787   ATTN: Mr. de Haas